LIBRARY OF MONEY AND BANKING HISTORY

# CONSIDERATIONS
ON
COMMERCE
*BULLION AND COINS*
CIRCULATION AND EXCHANGES

Also Published in

*REPRINTS OF ECONOMIC CLASSICS*

*By* GEORGE CHALMERS

THE COMPARATIVE STRENGTH OF GREAT BRITAIN [ 1794 ]

# CONSIDERATIONS

ON

# COMMERCE
# *BULLION & COINS*
# CIRCULATION AND EXCHANGES

BY

GEORGE CHALMERS

[1811]

REPRINTS OF ECONOMIC CLASSICS

AUGUSTUS M. KELLEY · PUBLISHERS
*NEW YORK 1969*

*FIRST EDITION 1811*

(London: Printed by Luke Hansard & Sons, *near Lincoln's-Inn Fields*, For J. J. Stockdale, *No. 41, Pall-Mall*, 1811)

Reprinted 1969 by

AUGUSTUS M. KELLEY · PUBLISHERS

*New York New York 10010*

---

Library of Congress Catalogue Card Number

68-55502

---

PRINTED IN THE UNITED STATES OF AMERICA

*by* SENTRY PRESS, NEW YORK, N. Y. 10019

# CONSIDERATIONS

ON

# COMMERCE,

# Bullion and Coin,

# CIRCULATION AND EXCHANGES;

WITH A VIEW TO

*OUR PRESENT CIRCUMSTANCES.*

BY GEORGE CHALMERS, F.R.S. S.A.

*THE AUTHOR OF*

THE COMPARATIVE STRENGTH OF GREAT BRITAIN;
&c.

" *I would not wish to have it understood, in the City, that*
" *this Court had* ANY DOUBT, *whether* BANK NOTES
" *be not always considered as* MONEY, *or* CASH."

LD. MANSFIELD.

LONDON:

Printed by Luke Hansard & Sons, near Lincoln's-Inn Fields,

FOR J. J. STOCKDALE, No. 41, PALL-MALL,

1811.

# ADVERTISEMENT.

WHEN I was preparing for the press a new Edition of my ESTIMATE, eight months ago, my attention was naturally drawn to the analogous topicks of Bullion and Coin, of Circulation and Exchanges, which then occupied the public attention, from the examinations of the *Bullion Committee.*

I also engaged in similar enquiries, in order to satisfy my own judgment on those difficult questions, in our existing circumstances of trade, at home, and transactions, abroad. I published my *Estimate*; and I drew up what I had to say on all those topicks, for future publication, before the Report of that Committee was given in, and, of course, before it was retailed, in Newspapers, and republished, as a Pamphlet.

But,

But, I have not found in it any facts, or seen any arguments, which have induced me, to change the opinions, that I had already formed, from my previous researches, and subsequent reflections. I have thought it necessary, to state the foregoing intimations, in this prefatory Advertisement; to account, for some of the *matter*, as well as the *manner* of the considerations, which I now submit to the Publick.

# CONSIDERATIONS

ON

## COMMERCE;

## *BULLION AND COIN*;

## CIRCULATION AND EXCHANGES.

DURING the progressive prosperity of Great Britain, in all that constitutes opulence, and power, throughout the effluxion of half a century, the year 1809 was the most prosperous.

This truth will, equally, appear, whether we consider our domestic industry, or our foreign trade. In that year of energy, the people of this country engaged in a thousand more enterprizes, within our several Shires, than they had ever done before, in any age of their efforts. There were, in fact, passed a greater number of laws, for local meliorations, than had ever been enacted, in the busiest period. Were we to examine the Parliamentary record, we should find that, in the eight years, which ended with 1809, there was a much greater number of such energizing statutes enacted, than in the eight years preceding; that

that in the eight years, which elapsed in 1800, there was a still greater number of such salutary laws made, in this period, than in the eight years, which ended in 1792. We may thus infer, from the public record, an important point of experience, that the vigorous people of this animated nation carry the struggle of war into their domestic pursuits. Owing to that augmented energy, there were more skill, more capital, and more people, employed in the labours of agriculture, during the busy year 1809, than any former period could boast: Nor, were there, in any age, more dividing of Commons, more inclosing of Wastes, more draining of Fens. When Excises, and such taxes, yield abundantly, this circumstance evinces the full employment of the people; their industrious pursuits, and their abilities to consume what their wants, or wishes, demand.

The exportation of vast cargoes, being the surplus products of such a people's labour, proves, sufficiently, that there must have been very extensive, and persevering industry at home, to produce such cargoes, for export abroad. This nation never enjoyed the advantages of so immense a foreign trade, as it happily possessed, in the memorable year 1809. The greatest export of any former time, was that of 1802, a year of peace, when we sent out the value of £.41,411,966: But, in 1809, a year of hostilities, after our commerce had been denounced, by the Berlin, and Milan decrees, we exported from Great Britain,

tain, the much more valuable cargo of £.50,301,763. Never, in any period, belonged to the several ports of this country so many ships: There were never, in any year, employed so many shipping, to transport such uncommon surpluses of what our land, and labour, produced. We may be said to have enjoyed, at the conclusion of that productive year, the whole trade, which the unhappy world retained; since we had possessed ourselves of the ships, commerce, and colonies of our malignant enemy. * It is, only Mr. Huskisson, who cries out, in the language of regret, when stating his question:

> " *I*, waking, view'd with grief the rising sun,
> " And fondly mourn'd *the dear delusion gone*."

It is of considerable importance, in answering such a question, amidst such regrets, to submit to the more cheerful reader the fair value, at which our prodigious commercial concerns might, in that year, be calculated:—

| | |
|---|---|
| The official value of the imports, and exports, in 1809, *exclusive* of the value of the imports, from India, and China, amounted to - - - - - - - | £. 80,708,823 |
| Add 50 per cent. for the difference between the real, and the official value - - - | 40,354,421 |
| Carried forward - | £. 121,063,244 |

* See, in the Appendix, a Chronological Account of Commerce, in this island, from the Restoration, to the end of 1809: I have annexed this comprehensive document; because it will support, with decisive strength, many of my considerations.

| | |
|---|---|
| Brought forward - | £. 121,063,244 |
| The domestic trade has always been deemed at least equal, if not superior, to our oversea trade; hence - - - - - - - | 121,063,244 |
| The coast trade may be estimated at one half of the imports, and exports; hence - - | 60,531,622 |
| | £. 302,658,110 |
| Add to the above the value of ships, which were registered, in Great Britain, in 1809; being 2,368,468 tons, at £. 10 per ton - - | 23,684,680 |
| The freight thereon, at £. 5 per ton - - | 11,842,340 |
| The difference, between the tonnage of British vessels, cleared inwards, and outwards, (3,070,725) for the year 1800, and the registered tonnage, as above, 2,368,468; being 702,257 tons, at £. 10 per ton - - - - - - - - | 7,022,570 |
| The freight thereon, at £. 5 per ton - - | 3,511,285 |
| | £. 348,218,985. |
| The amount of property insured, in 1809 - * | 162,538,900. |

Such, then, was the amount of the dealings of Great Britian, domestic, and foreign, during the year 1809, as laid before the House of Commons, by a very well-informed Committee †. From all those considerations, we may perceive, how much labour was put in motion, and sustained; how much commercial value was produced; and how many

* The basis of that Estimate was derived from the Computation of the Insurance Committee; and laid before the Commons house, in the last Session: See the Report of that able Committee.

† Id.

facilities

facilities were given to every man, and to every measure, by our *paper money*, which seems to be now discredited, at least, by all those, who, from habit, or accident, or association, look with malign aspect on our national prosperity: And hence, the recent efforts of mischief, the misconceptions of interest, and the falshood of disappointment; the publications of self-conceit, and the usual insidiousness of French œconomists:

> "Who can add colours ev'n to the Cameleon;
> "Change ſhapes with Proteus, *for advantage*."

As the heart, that sends out, and receives, the vital fluid, *the Bank*, which energizes our whole circulation, is regarded by those several classes, with jealous vigilance. By interest, the Bank is said to issue too few Notes: By factiousness, the Bank is charged with issuing too many Notes. When we see the wide-circulating journals of the South, and North, inculcate, with sly insidiousness, the positive depreciation of the Bank Notes; when we perceive pamphlet, after pamphlet, attempting to demonstrate the discredit of Bank cash; when we observe such frequent declamations, followed by serious enquiry; we may easily suppose, *there must be more meant, than meets the ear*. When the great end of the United Irishmen was to produce bloody change, in Ireland, by the overthrow of all government, and the destruction of all property, the directory

Directory of those miscreants recommended to their followers the refusal of the Bank of Ireland's Notes *. Such attempts, on the opposite sides of the Channel, by similar miscreants, evince a coincidence of mischief; and show, with sufficient conviction, the existence of the same design, to sap the foundations of the Bank, while they wish to weaken the stability of the State.

The year 1797 will always be memorable, in our commercial annals, for the well-known restriction of the Bank, by Parliament. This restriction was accompanied, by the secret enquiries of both Houses of Parliament. By them it was disclosed, that the Bank possessed a surplus of effects over her debts, of £. 3,839,550, *exclusive* of £. 11,526,350 sterling money, as the debt, from the Nation, to the Bank. This is plainly a satisfactory statement. The Bank Directors, by a memorable resolution, in October 1597, submitted to the wisdom of Parliament, their ability, and their willingness, to issue specie, for the public accommodation, according to

* The proceedings of the Secret Committees of the Irish Parliament record that malignant *fact*. Some years ago, when Jacobinism ran high, in Great Britain, I was assured, by a person, who knew the circumstance, that a leading Jacobin, at Manchester, went about the Exchange, there, offering Bank of England notes, at a discount: but, he was soon met, by very different persons, who, seeing his purpose, offered to take a £. 1,000, a week, at his discounts. This promptitude put an end to the Jacobin's impertinence.

their usual practice, "if *the political circumstances* "*of the Country* did not render it inexpedient." But, the Parliament were then actuated, by too much knowledge of our enemies' projects, and influenced by too much wisdom, to withdraw the restriction, which had been imposed, by circumspection, and has been continued, by experience. Thus are the affairs of the Bank, and the interests of the State, interwoven into the same web of policy; so that the tearing of the one might rend the other: And hence, may we perceive the maligners of the Bank, and the enemies of the State, to be generally the same; the same in object; the same in mischief; the same in means. Yet, will it, also, be memorable, in our commercial annals, that the year 1809, after that restriction had witnessed a dozen years prosperity, surpassed any former period, in national meliorations, domestic industry, and foreign trade *.

Such, however, are the wonderous changes of a changeful world! The most prosperous period is sometimes clouded, by a disastrous year: Many traders adventure out on the ocean of commerce, as I have, formerly, remarked; yet, all cannot return, with happy gales, into port. The year 1792 was the most remarkable of any former time, for industry at home, and traffick abroad: Yet, was it followed,

* See the Chronological Table, Appendix, N° 1. for the facts.

by

by the bankruptcies of 1793! The year 1809 was superior to 1792, in every thing, that constitutes superior industry, and more extensive commerce, in the proportion of £. 50,000,000, and upwards to £. 25,000,000; yet, was this prosperousness accompanied, by unfavourable exchanges, and followed by several bankruptcies; by some debility of public, and of private credit. But,—

> "Let us embrace those *sour adversities*:
> "For, wise men say, it is the wisest course."

It is, indeed, a fact, which cannot be doubted, that our Exchanges have, for some months, been unfavourable, amidst the commercial revolutions of the European world. Several of the most considerable towns, in Europe, whence Exchanges were carried on, under happier auspices, to a great extent, ceased to be commercial, when those *sour adversities* fell upon them. And the disadvantageous Exchanges with Hamburgh, Amsterdam, and France, are now attributed to every cause, except the true one. The first cause, that occurs to vulgar minds is a wrong balance upon our general trade. When we see exported, from Great Britain, during the busy year 1809, a cargo of the value of £. 50,301,761, according to the Custom-house books; when we are assured, that the real value, according to accurate computations, from the current prices, of that vast cargo, amounted to £. 66,017,712,

£. 66,017,712, sterling money, we may perceive, how many balances must be owing to us, on our general trade *. But, our traders give long credits; and such vast debts are not easily collected into the hands of their friends, abroad, to their use, while bills of exchange must be accepted: Yet, those great Exports plainly show how much the *balance of trade* is in favour of this Commercial island. While, however, the revolutionary system of the Continent continues to vex every European Prince, and to injure every industrious people; while the same system of vexation, and wrong, is applied to the British traffick, our foreign funds cannot be easily brought round to their true destination, either to liquidate debts, or to anticipate draughts: and we may owe balances to northern Europe, which are settled for at Hamburgh; whence the whole claims upon this nation are drawn for, in bills of exchange, or are acquitted to whatever amount, by the transmission of bullion, or goods. I have been assured by Hamburgh merchants, of great acuteness, and knowledge, who are in the daily habit of making remittances to that commercial town, that the real causes of *the lowness of the Exchanges*, with Hamburgh, and the export of bullion, undoubtedly are, that the present balance, not of *trade* but of *payments*, is against Great Britain; and those very intelligent merchants insist, whatever theorists may

* See the Chronological Table, Appendix, N° 1.

say,

say, that those overpowering payments have arisen, from the vast importations, during recent times, *from the Baltic*, which must be paid for, at Hamburgh, while goods cannot be sent thither, for preserving the equilibrium of the exchange. The facts, which have just been stated, by those, who feel the truth, represent our trade to the principal ports of Europe, as in a revolutionary state. We may easily perceive some of the effects of the Berlin Decree. And we may see very sufficient reason for doubting, whether the vast cargoes, which were exported, in 1809, to the European Continent, amounting to the real value of £. 27,190,000 sterling money, *all reached their destined ports.* Nor, did the circuitous trade of the American citizens, to Europe, furnish, in that year, many credits, or frequent remittances, as the proceeds of that commerce, to meet the bills of exchange, from the neighbouring Continent. We may now perceive two of the great causes, that produced the deficiency of British funds, on the neighbouring Continent, notwithstanding our vast exportations to Europe.

We come at length to the last, though not the least of the various causes, which have crippled our European trade, and narrowed our commercial funds, on the neighbouring Continent. The *Dominator of Europe* commands, that British merchants shall neither traffick, nor possess any such funds; that the products of British labour shall be destroyed. Such

Such a code requires not an elaborate commentary. The enforcement of such a code, from such a legislator, must necessarily obstruct the dealings of trade, and lessen the efficiency of credits, in Northern Germany: Under such an unrelenting tyranny, no one will be so hardy, or so foolish, as to avow, that he possesses either British goods, or British credits*. As the very principle of exchange is confidence, what exchanges can exist under a code of treachery! There is another cause, which has no small weight, in the present considerations: During the times, that are passed, various commercial cities existed, which made exchanges, and re-exchanges, to a great extent; such as Venice, Leghorn, and Genoa, in the South; in the North, the Hanse-towns: By carrying on, through their means, circuitous exchanges, the direct exchanges were greatly facilitated, and particular pressures somewhat eased. But, where are now the *Free Towns* of the South, or North! We may say, with a little departure from the original thought, and expression:

> " Their good stars, that were our former helps,
> " Have empty left their orbs, and shot their fires
> " Into the abysm of hell!"

Such, then are the real causes of our unfavourable exchanges, and the consequent export of bul-

* We have heard, lately, from Altona, and its neighbourhood, that, under the Napoleon code of commerce, the wife betrays her husband, the son his father, brother impeaches brother, and the friend his friend.

lion,

tion, which are quite equal to the distressing effects. But most of those causes are merely contemporary with the Continental System; and with it, their effects will of course disappear, when the patient prudence of the British merchants shall have performed their commercial engagements; with which, however, the Bank of England has certainly no direct concern.

That truth may be demonstrated, from a brief history of the *Bank Restriction.* The origin of this salutary measure is not to be attributed to the desires of the Bank Directors; but, to the prudence of Government, and the wisdom of Parliament. The epoch of that Restriction is February 1797, and, the state of the Nation, at that epoch, may be shortly given, in the following manner: The whole Exports of Great Britain amounted, in that year, to £. 28,917,010; and the balance of trade to about £. 7,906,000. The sum of Bank Notes, which was then circulated, for the common benefit, may be stated at £. 10,403,000. There were coined, in 1797, £. 2,000,297 of gold; while the price of standard silver was 5/2½ per ounce. The exchange with Hamburgh was 36. 9; and the 3 Per Cent. Consols sold, on an average, at 53¼ per cent. Under all those circumstances, at the end of 1797, the Bank Directors submitted to Parliament their ability, and willingness, to pay, as usual,

usual, in specie, *if the wisdom of the nation* saw *no political* reason to prevent them.

But, the wisdom of Parliament did see *political reasons*, in the nature of the war, and the malignity of our enemy, to enforce the Restriction, rather than relinquish the gold to such an enemy. And, during the second year of the Bank Restriction, notwithstanding all that orators could say, or pamphleteers could write, there occurred a vast flow of trade, favourable exchanges, cheap silver, and every appearance of general prosperity;—except, that the *Bank Issues* had risen, as a necessary consequence of locking up the gold coins, from £.10,403,000 to £.12,695,970: Yet, are there wise men, who think, such an additional issue may have contributed somewhat to the said prosperity. Meantime, *money* abounded, which, in some minds, is the *great good*: and, this favourable state of commercial matters, during this *second year* of the *Bank Restriction*, was attributed "to the balance of trade." In this prosperous year, 1798, "it was ascertained, by the "most accurate enquiries, that there was a profit on "bullion, by importing, and selling, *at the mint* "*price*; so advantageous was the Exchange owing "to the *favourable balance* of trade with this "country: The great influx of gold, and silver, into "this island, since February 1797, being wholly "owing to that favourable circumstance, in our "Commercial affairs; and there being, at the same "time,

" time, to counteract that influx, no payment of any " foreign loans, or subsidies, or extraordinary ex- " pences, incurred in other countries :" Add to the foregoing representation : " Every Hamburgh packet " continued [in 1798] to import into this country " a large quantity of gold; much was thus im- " ported, in the natural course of trade; and con- " siderable sums were imported, by commission, " from *the Bank*,"—

" While those halcyon days brought forth the arts of Peace."

Such, then, was the favourable state of money matters, throughout the prosperous year 1798, notwithstanding the *Bank Restriction!* The exchange with Hamburgh, in that year, vibrated from 38. 2. to 37. while the average rate of the whole year was about 37. 7½.; which is full 11⅔ per cent. in favour of Great Britain. A favourable exchange of 11⅔ per cent. produced, as we have seen above, that great current of bullion, by every packet; there being no adverse circumstances of *loans* or *subsidies*, to foreign powers, to check the fulness, and rapidity of its flow *. But, is it not

* The Bank Issues fluctuated, in 1798, from £. 12,000,000 to £. 13,000,000. There was, in that year, an export of bullion to our factories abroad of £. 1,264,287, which we may infer had little, or no effect, while the current of bullion set in, with such abundant influx. The balance of trade, to which such great effects were attributed, as it appeared, on the Custom-house books, was only £. 5,743,888: But, the favourable exchange was 11⅔ per cent. above *the par*.

not apparent, from those proofs, that if a *favourable* exchange of 11⅔ per cent. produced so great an *inward* current, an *unfavourable* exchange of 11⅔, equally unchecked, by any collateral circumstances, would, in the same manner, produce an *outward* current of bullion of equal flow, and fulness. Now the average of the adverse exchanges of 1809, being 11½ per cent, below par, what must have been the current of bullion exported! This deduction seems to decide the whole question, concerning the cause, and the effects, of the exchanges, in 1809.

But, at the end of 1798, a sad reverse was at hand. Though the exchange continued thus favourable, during the four first months of 1799; yet, before the end of this year, the exchange had fallen, against this country, to 32; and the price of standard silver rose from 5/1 to 5/4½ per ounce. Those great effects are attributed, by Mr. Mushet, and Lord King, to the enlarged issue of Bank notes, from £. 12,695,970, to £. 13,397,820. But, what do collateral facts, and instructive circumstances, prove? *Foreign subsidies*, and *bad seasons*, began now to shed their unhappy influences, on our *political economy*. The *dear years*, 1799, 1800, and 1801, demanded an export of twenty millions of specie *: And other adverse circumstances produced debilitating

* The Minister said in Parliament, on the 3d of February 1803; "We have had three years of *scarcity*, during which, "twenty

debilitating effects on the exchanges with Hamburgh, and incidentally, on the bullion market of our island. The average exchange with Hamburgh, during the first six months of 1799, being 36. 6½, was 8½ per cent. above *the par* of 33. 8; and the average of the last six months of the same year, being 33. 2. was nearly 1½ per cent. below the same *par* *. The average exchange, with Hamburgh, of the year 1800, being 31. 8. was nearly 6 per cent. *below* par: And the average of 1801 being 31. 7. was 6⅕ per cent. *below* par †. The flourishing trade, to which the Minister alluded, when he delivered his sentiments, on the said 3d of February 1803, were the exports of the years 1800, 1801, and the year of peace, 1802;

" twenty millions of specie have been sent out of this coun-
" try, for the purchase of Corn: There has been also a
" drain of specie, in consequence of larger sums of money being
" sent out of the kingdom, for the payment of our army, and
" navy, in the several parts of the world. We have, it is true,
" a flourishing commerce; but, it has not yet had the effect of
" bringing back the specie, thus drawn from the Country."

* It was given in evidence to the Lords Committee, during the Enquiry of 1797, by those who knew the best, that 33. 8. for the pound sterling is the *par* of Exchange with Hamburgh, according to the usage of many years; and that Castaign's Papers are calculated on this *par*.

† The fame persons gave in evidence to the Lords' Secret Committee, 1797, " that the exchange at 33. to 33.6. will " carry bullion out of this country; and when, from 36. to 36.6. " it will bring in bullion: the price of gold, generally *falling*, " when the exchange *rifes*; and the price of gold *rifing*, when " the exchange *falls*; in the abfence of extraordinary caufes."

but

but, in all those years of *great export*, the *course* of Exchange was *adverse* to this country*. Such, then, were the facts, which the Minister had within his contemplation, on the 3d of February 1803: When he spoke of our flourishing trade, there were greater cargoes exported, in those three preceding years, than had ever been sent, from this industrious country before: And yet, were the exchanges unfavourable, during the same three years, though one of them was a year of peace. But did the gradual rise of the Bank issues create the unfavourable exchanges of those times? Or, was it the remittances of Specie, and the Subsidies, that were stated by the finance Minister? The great issues of the Bank in 1802, were demanded by the industry, and exports of that peaceful year, when the Bank sustained the labours, and promoted the commerce of our ener-

| | The Exports: | The Exchange: | The Bank issues: |
|---|---|---|---|
| * In 1800, | £. 38,120,120; | *below* par, 6 p$^r$ c$^t$; | -£. 14,563,740. |
| In 1801 - | 37,786,857; | - d$^o$ - 6$\frac{1}{6}$ p$^r$ c$^t$; | - 15,459,050. |
| In 1802 - | 41,211,966; | - d$^o$ - 2$\frac{1}{3}$ p$^t$ c$^t$; | - 16,320,958. |

Add to those instructive Statements, that there was laid before the Parliament, on the 29th of June 1801, a Treasury Account; showing the amount of the several sums of money advanced, by way of loan, or subsidy, to the different States, from the beginning of the war, to have been £. 12,599,288. 2. 10.; against all which the Bank Directors constantly remonstrated, as producing *unfavourable* exchanges. Those several facts, converging to one point, prove, that the *Bank issues* did not produce the *unfavourable exchanges*; but tended to support the exchanges, by facilitating a *great export* of goods.

getic

getic country. But, it may be again asked, were those remittances of specie, the effects of scarcity, and the result of subsidies, owing to the *Bank Restriction*; or did the *Bank issues* alleviate the one, and facilitate the other, when they sustained the industry, and promoted the exports of our enterprizing people! *

The reader was troubled with those details; as they are the very essence of the present enquiry: Those details are of so much importance, that every judicious reader must wish, for some further illustration, from different points of view. The Merchants, Bankers, and Brokers, who were examined by the Secret Committees of Parliament, in 1797, concurred in their opinions, that the favourable, or unfavourable exchanges, rule the money market; and ought to over-rule foreign subsidies; as they turn the balance of *payments* against this country; and the *balance of payments govern* the *exchanges*, while the commercial world is free, from domination.

* The war was renewed, in 1803: and, the first impressions of it were to reduce the exports of the country, from £.41,411,966 to £.31,438,495. The Bank issues of 1803 were somewhat less: The Hamburgh exchanges rose *above* par 1½ per cent.: and the price of bullion *fell* somewhat, as the exchange *rose*. Such was the commercial state of our affairs, when the various statutes, that had been made, from time to time, for confirming, and continuing the *Bank Restriction*, were, on the 15th of December 1803, after mature consideration of recent experience, *continued, during the war*, by the 44 Geo. III. ch. 1.

tion*. All the intelligent Merchants, and Brokers, with whom I have lately spoken, for my own information, concur in the several opinions, which have just been mentioned. Feeling their force, and the effects of a low, or high exchange, the Governors of the Bank heard, with a sort of horror, of a foreign loan. Yet, is the Minister obliged, amidst such wars, to make such loans, and to grant such subsidies; conceiving it to be far wiser, to fight such an enemy on the Rhine, and the Danube, on the Mondego, and Tagus, rather than the Thames, or the Shannon †.

It

* The late Mr. Giles, the Governor of the Bank, said to the Lords' Committee, in 1797: "I conceive, that *all loans*, made "for foreign Powers, or monies given to them, must ultimately "go in *specie*, although not remitted, in money; but, it "affects the exchange; so as to occasion gold to go out of the "country:"—and, being asked, If *the loan* would ultimately *go in specie, unless the exchange were reduced* BELOW *par*; he answered, pointedly: "It would *bring the exchange below par*."

† On the 6th of June 1799, a message was delivered, from the King, to Parliament, "that he had engaged with the Em-"peror of Russia, for 45,000 men; and for the fitting out of "which were to be given £.225,000; and, moreover, a "monthly subsidy of £.75.000:" And, among the Supplies, there were voted to the Emperor, as a subsidy, £.825,000.—On the 17th of February 1800, the Minister said, the total amount of the subsidy, which was wanted, for the German princes, would probably rise to £.2,500,000; but, he would only then move, for an advancement of £. 500,000. Now; such were the fluctuations of 1799, owing to those notices, that the Hamburgh exchange fell from 11⅞ per cent. *above* par to 6$\frac{5}{12}$ per cent.

It is a point agreed, then, from the experience of the past, and the facts of daily life, that every measure, which tends to raise *the balance* of *payments* against this country, necessarily brings down the exchange to unfavourable vibrations, and carries out our bullion, whatever can be opposed to its issue. We see additional proofs of this, in the singular state of our commerce, during 1809. There was a vast export of merchandize, far beyond the example of all former years, amounting in 1809 * to upwards of £. 66,000,000. of real value;

cent. *below* par: and, notwithstanding the great exportations of the years 1800, and 1801, the exchange, in the first, was 6 per cent. *below* par; and in the second year, 1801, continued *below* par $6\frac{1}{6}$ per cent.: Nay; though the peace was, at length, made; and 1802 was a year of extraordinary export; yet, the exchange of 1802 was still $2\frac{1}{3}$ per cent. *below* par. Those facts, and circumstances, convert the *reasonings* of Mr. Giles into *experience*. When the vast exports of 1802, however, were brought round upon the balance of *payments*, in 1803, the exchange with Hamburgh rose to be $1\frac{2}{3}$ per cent. *above* par: and, in the hostile years, 1804-5-6-7 and 1808, the exchanges, owing to our great trade, in the absence of foreign loans, continued *above* the par. It was the vast imports, of 1809, with the obstruction of remittances, owing to the revolutionary causes, before mentioned, which converted those *favourable* exchanges to a *ruinous exchange* of $11\frac{1}{2}$ per cent. *below* the par, that nothing, but the great credit, and resources of this country, could withstand.

* The *real* value of Exports, from Great Britain, as we learn, from the Bullion Report, 228,
was, in 1805, £. 51,109,131; - in 1806, £. 53,028,881;
in 1807, £. 50,482,661; - in 1808, £. 49,969,746;
in 1809, £. 66,117,712, sterling money.

there

there was an immense balance on our general trade with the world, amounting to £. 14,884,649 of real value*: And yet, a most extraordinary import, from the North of Europe, in that year, turned the balance of payments, in favour of Hamburgh; while revolutionary means were employed, on the neighbouring continent, to prevent the funds of the importers, from reaching their friends, in that great emporium. We see, accordingly, every thing, that was given in evidence to the Parliament of 1797, by the Merchants, Bankers, and Brokers, in full operation; The exchange fell BELOW par to 11½ per-cent.; and bullion was sent out, at whatever price; to answer the unfavourable balance of *payments*, between the North of Europe and England. The foregoing facts, and circumstances, then, are adequate causes, to produce the disadvantageous effects of an adverse exchange of 11½ per-cent.; of the export of gold and silver; and of the consequent rise of the prices of bullion, in the markets at home†.

Thus,

* According to a castigated account of the Inspector General, in the Bullion Report, 228, the real balance of our trade with all the world,
was, in 1805, £. 6,616,434; - in 1806, £. 10,433,727;
in 1807, £. 5,866,944; - in 1808, £. 12,481,290;
in 1809, £. 14,884,649.

† In addition to all those facts, reasonings, and accounts, I will beg leave to state a detail, from Sir Francis Baring's *Observations*, 1797: In speaking, p. 49, of the exchanges with Hamburgh,

Thus, then, according to Sir Francis Baring, there is no occasion to ask a question of the Bullion Committee, with regard to those practical points, when there is an adverse exchange of 11½ per-cent.: We are therefore, justified, in saying, if the revolutionary system of the Dominator of Europe should cease, what has happened in our commercial affairs, would again happen:

> " ——————The hearts
> " Of all his people may revolt from him,
> " and kiss the lips of unacquainted change."

---

Hamburgh, 1796, he proved, by calculation, that there was then a profit on exporting *gold* to Hamburgh,

in January 1796 - of - 7½ per cent.;
in February 1796 - of - 6½ per cent.;
in March 1796 - of - 8⅜ per cent.:

After thus showing such profits, on the export of bullion, Sir Francis cried out: " With such documents, in the possession " of every foreign Merchant, there is no occasion to ask a " question, either of the Treasury, or of the Bank."—" It " must be indifferent," he adds, " if bullion be exported, to " what service it shall be applied; but, it is of infinite im- " portance, whether the magnitude of the sum shall exceed, " or fall short of the balance of trade; for whilst the balance " of trade is favourable, the money must return." I concur entirely with that eminent merchant, in his reasonings, as applied to our commercial affairs, in 1809: on our general trade, we had a great balance: but, owing to those revolutionary measures, our funds were prevented from meeting our debts, payable in the North of Europe: and thereby the exchange fell to be unfavourable, 11½ per cent.; yet, while the balance of *trade* is in our favour, the money must return: We have seen how it returned in 1798, soon after the Bank Restriction took place, when the exchange rose 10 per cent. in our favour; and how it flowed, in many subsequent years of war.

I.—Of

## — I. —

## Of the EXCHANGES.

We are thus conducted, by a regular progress, to the great question, whether those effects, of *unfavourable exchanges*, and *high prices of bullion*, be owing to causes at home, or to causes abroad; whether to the *revolutionary causes*, on the neighbouring Continent; *or*, to the *depreciation* of the *Bank paper*, from its supposed superabundance. I mean to maintain, that the true causes of those disadvantageous effects originated *abroad*, and *not* at home: And I shall argue the question from facts, from circumstances, and from experience, against all those, who treat a very important subject of daily life, from abstract principles, idle theories, and a bold defiance of common sense.

1. The first fact is, that we are at war; we are at war, with Bonaparte*: And the French troops, say the said Committee, *possess the North of Germany:* But, this is saying nothing, to the purpose; since the mere possession of the French troops, while they left every one to follow his own affairs, in his own way; to enjoy his pursuits, and his property; would not affect the exchange: It is, in this question, as in several sorts of cases, which come before our criminal courts, absolutely neces-

* It must always be remembered, that this was the great cause, which induced the wisdom of Parliament, in December 1803, to continue the Bank Restriction to the end of the war, and six months beyond it.

sary,

sary, to speak in plain terms: Bonaparte has declared, and his will is the law, that we shall have no trade in Europe; that we shall have no goods, nor credits, any where, within *his domination*, that we shall have no funds, and no remittances. These are facts, which are but too well known, and too much felt, all over Europe. Those facts go to the very soul of the question, as we see our traders can neither have credits, nor can they send cargoes, to meet demands. We see, then, from the foregoing considerations, how much more those revolutionary measures produce unfavourable exchanges, than the loans, and subsidies, which, as we have seen, produced unfavourable exchanges, and drained this country of bullion, by enabling the foreign Powers, to draw bills on this Nation, to the amount of the loans, or subsidies; and thereby augmenting the balance of payments: But, the merchants met those payments, by *the export* of *goods*, which preserved the equable balance of exchanges, while goods could be sent. The wonder now is, when we see such tyranny, aided too by treachery, applied to our commercial transactions, that any sort of exchanges should remain. Are we then to enquire, why the Hamburgh exchange has fallen to 11½ per cent.; why our bullion should be exported; why bullion is uncommonly dear, in the market of London!

2. While our traders were thus deprived of their funds, their credits, and their correspondencies, and

of

of the various means of meeting payments, great importations were made, from the North of Europe*. To satisfy such vast demands, there appears to have been no other resource but drawing bills upon this country, at a very reduced exchange of schillings and grotes, for our pound sterling. They very naturally sent bullion to Hamburgh, even at a high price, till the bullion was exhausted. It is asked, with more acuteness, than experience, since a hundred pounds, in specie, may be transported to Hamburgh, at the expence of £. 3. 12. 11. why not send bullion, rather than incur the loss of an adverse exchange of 11½ per cent. The proper answer is, that there was not adequate bullion to send. If there had been bullion, to remit, from the London market, to Hamburgh, it would have been intercepted, and condemned, as the property

* A very eminent, and well informed Russia merchant has informed me, as follows: "In the year 1809, we imported, "from Russia, produce of the value of £.5,000,000 sterling, "at least; for which we paid £. 4,000,000 sterling in *freights* "to neutral ships, or such as are called neutral: what came "from other *Baltic* ports, I don't know; but, our importa- "tions, from Russia, relieved that country of an immense "load, which cost this nation about what I have said." Mr. Greffulhe gave pretty much the same information to the Bullion Committee. Minutes, 64, of the 8° edit. Those intimations are confirmed, by a castigated account of the Inspector General, that we imported, from Europe, in 1808, £. 8,905,099, and £. 19,821,601, in 1809, of *real value:* This statement of those two years, though the *imports* were, from all Europe, evinces, incidentally, what a vast amount must have been imported, from the *Baltic.*

of

of English traders. Nor, was it possible, amidst those commercial embarrassments, to make circuitous remittances, by drawing on, and remitting to other towns, which would have sustained the direct exchanges: The middlemen too, or exchangers, were gone; and the very *free towns*, the busy scenes of trade, and the very seats of exchangers, had ceased to be commercial. Again; while our trade, with Hamburgh, remained free, and the exchange became adverse, every merchant knew, how to profit from both those circumstances: When, from the state of the exchanges, he saw, that he must receive a smaller number of schillings and grotes, for his pound sterling, he perceived, incidentally, that the price of goods, in the London market, was lessened, in proportion, to the fall of the exchange: And of course, by making his remittance to Hamburgh, in goods, in preference to bullion, he not only saved the loss on the exchange, but obtained a profit on the goods exported. Such was the practice of merchants! But, could this operation, which was so familiar, and so frequent, while trade was free, be performed, in 1809? No: and of course the whole exchanges, and the prices of bullion, became disorganized, when the usual expedient of sending cheaper cargoes, which kept both the *course* of the *exchange*, and *the prices* of *bullion*, in *equilibrium*, could no more be applied. Moreover, it has been intimated to me, by a very respectable merchant, who

who is well acquainted with foreign affairs, that the *non-exportations* of the American trade may bear, considerably, on this question; as the British creditors were thereby deprived of *credits*, on the neighbouring continent: The American citizens are always indebted ten, or twelve millions, to the British merchants, for goods furnished on credit, which the American citizens were in the habit of paying, by the consignment of their ships, and cargoes, to their correspondents, in Europe, who were directed by them, to remit the proceeds to their British creditors *. From that important information, we may again perceive the sophistry of arguing abstract propositions, without adverting to special circumstances, which are the essential facts of the case: And, this examination brings us round to the main questions, why are the exchanges *so low*, and the price of bullion *so high?* The pointed answer, among sound reasoners, must be; because revolutionary means were interposed, to prevent the usual application of the appropriate *equilibrium* of *goods*.

3. If we take a different view of this litigated question, we shall distinctly perceive, whether the rising, or falling of the exchange be owing to the *revolutionary causes*, before mentioned, or to the *Bank issues*, which the Committee supposes. The

* The well-informed Mr. Greffulhe gave pretty much the same information, I see, to the Bullion Committee. Minutes, 68, of the 8° edit.

epoch

epoch of the Bank Restriction was February 1797, as we have seen; and 1809 was the 13th year of the Restriction, amidst wars, and subsidies. Let us now see, how the Exchanges stood, whether favourable, or adverse, in each year:

| | | Above par. — | Below par. |
|---|---|---|---|
| In 1797, the Hamburgh Exchange | was | 9 1/8 p^r cent. | |
| In 1798 - - - - - D° - - | was | 11 2/3 p^r cent. | |
| In 1799 - - - - - D° - - | was | 4 p^r cent. | |
| In 1800 - - D° - - | was - - - - | | 6 p^r cent. |
| In 1801 - - D° - - | was - - - - | | 6 1/8 p^r cent. |
| In 1802 - - D° - - | was - - - - | | 2 1/5 p^r cent. |
| In 1803 - - - - - D° - - | was | 1 2/3 p^r cent. | |
| In 1804 - - - - - D° - - | was | 5 3/7 p^r cent. | |
| In 1805 - - - - - D° - - | was | 3 3/7 p^r cent. | |
| In 1806 - - - - - D° - - | was | 1 1/2 p^r cent. | |
| In 1807 - - - - - D° - - | was | 2 1/2 p^r cent. | |
| In 1808 - - - - - D° - - | was | 1 1/2 p^r cent. | |
| In 1809 - - D° - - | was - - - - | | 11 1/2 p^r cent. |
| Favourable - | | 9 years. | Adverse 4 years. |

It thus appears that, during the effluxion of 13 years, *under* the *Bank Restriction*, while more than a thousand domestic improvements were made, while extensive industry prevailed at home, and our trade to foreign parts prospered, beyond example, there were *nine* years of favourable, and *four* of adverse exchanges; the first being *above* par, and the last set of exchanges *below* par. What, then, is the fair conclusion, from the premises? That the *Bank Restriction* has shed a salutary, or a malign influence,

influence, on our commercial affairs; In *nine* years of favourable exchanges, the influence of the Bank was *salutary*; in the *four* years of adverse exchanges, we are to suppose it to have been *malign*. We have seen above, in 1797, and 1798, the two first years of that Restriction, how favourable the exchanges were; and we have already learned, from minute enquiries, how much bullion flowed into this country, as the consequences of those favourable exchanges, in 1797, and 1798. Then followed the three *dear years*, which cost the nation twenty million of specie, while there were *subsidies*, and *loans*, to aggravate that evil, and to augment that drain. At length, came the peace of 1802, which dragged after it the *long tail* of all wars, the settling of outstanding claims, and the funding of floating debts. The war was renewed in 1803, which was followed, by four hostile years of prosperous trade, and favourable exchanges, whatever may have been paid in *subsidies* to unsuccessful Allies. Sustained by the discounts of the restricted Bank, the Traders carried on a beneficial commerce, amidst malignant hostilities. And, it was the Berlin decree, and its consequent force, and perfidies, which reduced the favourable exchange of 1808 to 1½ per cent. and lowered the adverse exchange of 1809, to the extent of 11½ per cent. From this view of causes, and effects, I am led to say, in the true temper of Sir Francis Baring, that there is no occasion, with

this

this experience, and those facts, before us, to go to any set of men to ask, whether the *low* exchanges, and the *high* prices of bullion, in 1809, be owing to the Bank Restrictions of Parliament; to the revolutionary measures of the *Dominator* of Europe; or to *the depreciation of the current money.* General experience, and common sense, attribute the adverse exchanges, and high prices of bullion, to the revolutionary measures, beforementioned, with their attendant circumstances: The Bullion Committee has attributed the high price of bullion, and the unfavourable exchanges to *the depreciation of the current money*, in opposition to this common sense, and to that general experience *. It follows of course, from *the theory* of the Committee, that our

* The daily transactions of the *clearing-house*, in the City, where persons meet to settle their mutual claims of many millions, are in evidence, before the Bullion Committee. It is a fact, that bills of exchange are, every day, settled there, to the amount of five millions, without even aſking a single question about the price of guineas, or the depreciation of money, which price and depreciation, from intuition, they know to be imaginary; and without the intervention of Bank notes, except, for paying the small balance remaining unliquidated, that may be compared to the petty cash of common change. Would it not be rather ridiculous, in our pamphleteers, whether noble, or ignoble, to go into the said *clearing-house*, in order to warn the persons there assembled, at 4 o'clock, how they settle those vast transactions, without enquiring about the real value of guineas, the price of bullion, and above all, about the depreciation of money, which is supposed to rule the course of exchange, by the said pamphleteers.

current

current money was *depreciated*, during those *four* years of adverse exchanges, but, was *enhanced*, during the *nine* of favourable exchanges, under the *thirteen* years of the Bank Restriction. According to *that theory*, the current money rose, and fell in its value, from change of circumstances; and the exchanges rose, and fell, as a consequence: And thus, according to the same theory, *money* can no longer be counted a *standard*, since it varies with every wind, which brings in the mails. We have lived to see *mataphysicks* over-ruled by *common sense*: And, it requires not prophecy to foretell, that commercial practice, as it has always done, will continue to over-rule that *metaphysical theory*. The daily practice of the *clearing-house* derides all abstract theories, as useless, or pernicious.

4. Considering the foregoing facts, with their attendant circumstances, the practice of merchants, and the experience of business, the proposition, which attributes those adverse exchanges, and consequent prices of bullion, to the revolutionary measures of the Continental system, seems to be demonstrated: All those, indeed, who disregard facts, and circumstances, in their reasonings, who deride the practice of merchants, and the experience of business, of course conclude, from their scholastic conceits, that the unfavourable exchanges, and the dearness of bullion, arose from the Bank Restriction,

tion, while the sophisters were ignorant that, by the established law, *Bank Notes are Cash* *.

5. The same Sophists, who pretend, that Bank Notes are depreciated, because gold, and silver, are dear; in the same strain of sophistry insist, that Bank Notes are depreciated; because the exchanges are unfavourable: Now, from this sort of logic, we may infer, that since Bank Notes are supposed to be depreciated, when the exchanges are *low*, the same Bank Notes will become precious, when the exchanges become high: What, then, is this, but to make the value of Bank Notes to depend on a standard, which, from its fluctuations, is the most unlike a standard: The absurdity of this pretence consists, in trying to measure the value of Bank Notes, which have the permanence of *cash*, by exchanges, which have none. Money is said to be the *measure* of merchandizes; how, then, can exchanges, which rise, and fall, every post, be the measure of money? What is this mode of reasoning, but to make the fluctuations of exchange to be the standard measure of the money unit, or pound sterling, which are no longer to remain stationary, but, to vary with the fluctuations of the exchange †.

* See Mr. Huskisson's pamphlet.

† We may learn, from the very intelligent Harris, "that "*bills of exchange*, being substitutes for bullion, are *themselves* "as much a *commodity*, as *bullion*, or any thing else." Essay on Money, 128.

And,

And, we may thus perceive, from so absurd an argument, that exchanges, owing to their mutability, cannot be the *measure* of any thing; as bills of exchange are as much commodities, as merchandize: "These "observations, plainly, show, says Harris, the ablest "assay-master, in Europe, that any calculation of "national *profit*, or *loss*, from *the course of exchange*, must needs be very precarious:" yet, he adds, "is it almost certain, that by those transactions, the country will sustain some loss, against "which, the exchange bears; and, there is no *other* "*way of bringing the balance even, but by the exportation of goods*, or *bullion* *." Do not all the merchants say, that *the export of goods* is the best *equilibrium* of the unfavourable exchange? What would that assayist have thought of a proposal, which had a necessary tendency, to transfer the whole coins of a country, in favour of a malignant enemy, I pretend not to know.

6. The first person, who, during late times, tried to prove the depreciation of Bank notes, or cash, by

* Harris on Coin and Money, Commerce, and Exchanges, 1757, p. 123. Sir James Stuart, the profound political oeconomist, who knew Harris, personally, says that he was "the "best assay maker, in Europe." His Essay on Money evinces, that Harris was one of the most judicious writers, in Europe, with regard to the present question, though he did not live to see, what we have seen, a Continental system substituted. for a commercial system; the first founded upon force, and fraud; the second founded on freedom, and confidence.

a reference

a reference to the course of exchange, with all its fluctuations, was Lord King*. His Lordship supposed, probably, that foreign exchanges are estimated, and settled, on the *golden guinea*, and that the drawers of such bills, from abroad, expect to be paid, for their bills, in bullion. His Lordship was thus induced to collect a series of exchanges, which he compared, with contemporary issues, of Bank notes. And, seeing, as he supposed, that a large issue of Bank notes was generally accompanied, by an unfavourable exchange, he was thus led to think, that he could prove, from the course of the exchanges, the depreciation of Bank notes. But, are his Lordship's suppositions founded, in any thing but mistake! With Hamburgh, the exchanges are all made upon the *money unit*, or *pound sterling*, by demanding, and receiving an uncertain number of schellings and grotes, for the pound sterling: and the Hamburgh merchants entering into such transactions of exchange, expect to be paid, not in *bullion*, or in guineas, but in current money: The Hamburgh merchants have long known, that *Bank notes*, being *cash*, according to the custom of trade, and the common law, are a legal acquittal of such bills; that the current coins of this country, whether weighty, or light, could be of little use to them abroad; since they could neither export, nor melt such current

* His Lordship had the goodness to publish his *Thoughts*, in May 1803, a very inauspicious moment.

coins:

coins: Nor, do the Hamburgh merchants ever expect to be paid *in bullion*, which is a mere mercantile commodity, that rises, and falls, in its price, according to the demand, and the supply, in the market. We have already seen, how little the persons, who meet at the Clearing-house, in the City, with bills to be liquidated, think about bullion, or money, or any thing but currency, whether Bankers' cheques, or Bank notes. His Lordship, assuming thus, as the ground of his argument, what could not be supported, in fact, gave an imperfect book to the reading world. This will ever be the case with those, who deviate into abstractions, rather than delight to argue, from facts. His Lordship was soon refuted, by Mr. Henry Boase, with great superiority of knowledge, as well as vigour of reasoning. It was now clearly shown, that the Hamburgh exchanges had been different, in fact, from what his Lordship had supposed; that the Hamburgh merchants never expect to be paid their bills of exchange, contrary to their contract, in current *coins*, but, in the current *money* of Great Britain. Mr. Boase's argument, which proved, that the recoinage of the gold, from 1773, to 1777, inclusive, did not affect the exchanges, was nevertheless neglected, while Lord King's notions were followed, though his argument had been refuted.

7. Some persons of greater rank, and perhaps of superior talents, to Lord King, were misled, in their opinions,

opinions, as to the effects of the recoinage of the gold, from 1773 to 1777, by not adverting to the difference, between the *par* of exchange, and the *course* of exchange: All that can be allowed to those eminent persons is, that a good coinage is better than a bad coinage. The melioration of the guineas may have meliorated the *par* of exchange; but, certainly not the *course* of exchange, which is a quite different thing *. Now, those who speculate upon the effects of the recoinage, fail egregiously, in their argument, by not showing, that there was a new *par* of exchange settled with Hamburgh, in consequence of that melioration of the guineas: They could not show what never, in fact, happened †. And,

* See Mr. Boase's Letter to Lord King, 51. wherein he exhibits the Hamburgh exchanges, both before, and after that recoinage; and thereby demonstrates, that the exchanges were higher *before* that operation, which began in August 1773, than they were, during the eighteen months, which succeeded: for the Hamburgh exchange was 34.11, in March 1773, and never rose so high, throughout the subsequent months to the close of 1776. It is a fallacy to suppose, that the recoinage was made in one year: In 1773. there was only coined the sterling value of £. 1,317,645, which could not have much affected either the exchanges, or the price of bullion.

† Mr. de Mattos, the exchange broker, who, when he was examined by the Lords' Committee, [1797] had been four and thirty years, in that employment, [from 1763] did not recognize any such change of *par*; but spoke of it as fixed, at 33 schellings, and 8 grotes, for £. 1. sterling, both being mere money of account, and not *coins*. Mr. Eliason, another very experienced

And, those facts, and circumstances, evince, that the exchanges of Hamburgh are carried on, with less attention to the *coinage*, than some suppose, and with more regard to the *currency*, than others unwillingly allow. Those intimations strike very deep into the theory, which supposes the high exchanges

experienced broker of exchanges, concurred with M. de Mattos, on that occasion. We may now infer, that the speculators on the effects of the recoinage upon the exchange, are equally unfounded, in their fact, as they are absurd, in their reasoning; as all reasonining is, which contradicts fact, and experience. The subjoined Statement of Hamburgh Exchanges, which are submitted *tablewise* to the intelligent reader, will demonstrate the truth of what has been said above:

HAMBURGH EXCHANGES:

| In | 1770. | 1771. | 1772. | 1773. (recoinage.) | 1774. (recoinage.) | 1775. Do. | 1776. Do. |
|---|---|---|---|---|---|---|---|
| January - - | 33.2½ | 33.8⅓ | 32.7¾ | 34.1½ | 34.9¼ | 34,3 | 33.11½ |
| February - | 33.2 | 33.8⅝ | 32.9⅞ | 34.9¼ | 34.9 | 34.3½ | 33.10 |
| March - - | 33.2 | 33.7 | 32 11¾ | 34.11 | 34.9½ | 34.5 | 33.9 |
| April - - - | 33.3 | 33.6½ | 32.11⅓ | 34.9⅞ | 34.7⅝ | 34.4½ | 33.7 |
| May - - - | 33.3 | 33.4¾ | 32.10¾ | 34,10⅜ | 34.7⅔ | 34.3¼ | 33.6⅝ |
| June - - - | 33.1½ | 33.1¾ | 33.2⅝ | 34.9¾ | 34.8⅔ | 34.4½ | 33.4 |
| July - - - | 33.4 | 33.0¼ | 33.2⅔ | 34.10 | 35.8½ | 34.4¼ | 33.4½ |
| August - - | 33.4 | 32.11¾ | 33.4½ | 34.8⅝ | 34.6⅔ | 34.3⅔ | 33.4 |
| September - | 33.2¾ | 32.11¾ | 33.5¾ | 34.3¼ | 34.5 | 34.3⅙ | 33.5 |
| October - - | 33.3 | 32.10¼ | 33.9⅞ | 34.9 | 34.2 | 34.2⅔ | 33.2½ |
| November - | 33.4¾ | 32.8¾ | 33.9 | 34.8¾ | 34.3 | 34.2 | 33.2 |
| December - | 33.5½ | 32.7⅔ | 33.10½ | 34.9¼ | 34.3 | 34.0¾ | 33.1½ |
| Average of each year | 33.3 | 33.2¼ | 33.3 | 34.8¾ | 34.6½ | 34 3⅜ | 33.5⅝ |

of

of 1809, to be more owing to the Bank restriction, than to the Continental system.

8. As persons of great consideration have been thus led into misconceptions, on this important subject; it becomes necessary to enter into some ex-explanations, on the difficult topicks of foreign exchanges, about which so many volumes have been written, from the early days of Malynes and Missenden to the recent times of Muschet and Ricardo. The *par* in commerce is the equality, between different *coins*, in distant countries; so much as one must give of one sort of *specie*, for any other sort of *specie*: The *par* of exchange differs from the *course* of exchange, in this: The *par* shows what any other nation, or town, ought to allow in exchange; the *par* being *certain* and *fixed*, by the intrinsic values of the several *coins*, when estimated against each other: But, the *course* only shows what the exchangers *will allow*, in exchange; which is uncertain, and *contingent* *. There is another point, in this difficult

* See Chambers's Dict. in vo. *Par*. The late Joseph Harris, the well informed Assay-master of the Mint, wrote most distinctly, on this perplexing subject. Speaking of the *par* of exchange, he says, "the *monies* of the world are thereby, in "effect, reduced into one *common standard*; and, it may be "readily seen, how much of the *money* of one country is "equivalent to a given sum of another country." Essay on Money, 1757, p. 115. Mr. Muschet, one of the Clerks, in the Mint, who has favoured the world with *an enquiry* on *the effects of the Bank Restriction Act*, seems not to understand the *par* of exchange,

difficult subject, which the judicious Harris has solved. Some, he says, are apt to doubt, whether the exchange be favourable, or adverse, when they hear, that the exchange *falls* to our *loss*, and *rises* to our *gain*. The rule, he adds, is this; When the exchanges are made upon the *pound sterling*, as they are with Hamburgh, Holland, and Flanders, by receiving, for that *money unit* [£. 1.] which is a thing fixed, an uncertain number of schellings, and grotes, Flemish: And, the fewer of these, which are received for the *pound* sterling, the exchange is said to fall, in dis-favour of Great Britain. It is, however, quite different, continues he, when the exchange is made on the *money unit* of France, and Spain, or other countries, when we agree to give an uncertain number of our *pence*, for the *frank* of the one country, or the *dollar* of the other: And when we give more of our pence, for the frank, or piece of eight, than the *par* requires, the exchange is said to rise, in dis-favour of this country, and in favour of France, and Spain. Thus much, then, from the judicious, and intelligent Harris, for the better comprehending of the subject of exchanges, which is

exchange, in the same manner, that the Assay-master understood it; as something *fixed*, for a *standard*; since Mr. Muschet supposes a different *par* to exist every month; so that he confounds fixedness with *fluctuation*; and supposes *certainty*, and *uncertainty*, to exist in the *same* object: now; without a *standard*, there is no judging of the rise, or fall of the *course* of exchange, or whether it be favourable, or unfavourable.

undoubtedly

undoubtedly to those, who are unacquainted with such subjects, as obscure, as it is complex: But, the real practice of exchange, he concludes, branches out into an immense labarinth, which is not easily unfolded, without much experience, and attentive application. The general trader, however, without going into any labyrinth, and without any exposition, does understand, practically, the whole *course* of exchanges, with the commercial world, when it was not yet compressed, by revolutionary means. Such a trader watched the arrival of every mail, which exposed to his intelligent eyes, not the *par*, indeed, but *the course* of the exchanges, for the direction of his own affairs. If such a trader saw, that the *course* of the exchanges, by allowing so few schellings and grotes, for the pound sterling, was so low, as *to operate as a premium on* the *sending of goods* to the town, where the exchange was thus low; his next object of inspection was the whole prices current of merchandizes, in order to see what could, with the best effect, and the greatest profit, be sent thither: He now exported a cargo, so assorted, and to such an extent, as to bring the course of exchange to an *equilibrium.* Such was the true *anodyne* of an unfavourable exchange, till recent times. It was this operation of the traders, that enabled this country, by sending cargoes, in mitigation of the unfavourable exchange, to pay for the grain, which the dear years demanded; to aid, and subsidize

sidize foreign Princes; as well as to satisfy the whole demands, from the *stock* market, for *dividends*, and *transfers*: But, could such an operation be performed, to any advantage; could it be performed at all, during the unfavourable influences of the year 1809? Is it fair, then, in candid discussion, to investigate the question, without ascertaining every fact, and collecting every circumstance, which could, in any manner, bear upon the point at issue?

9. With this head of enquiry, as to *the course of exchange*, I have almost done. From the foregoing intimations, I am led to infer, in the face of what has been said, written, and reported, that whatever connection there may be, between the *par* of exchange, and *coins*, there is no necessary influence of cause and effect, between the *course* of exchange, and the *notes* of the Bank: For, the usual exchanges with Hamburgh are always settled, by a reference to the *money unit*, or *pound sterling*, as the standard; the Hamburgh Exchangers always expected to be paid in *the money of account*; as they knew, that the money of account was acquitted here in *Bank* notes, which, according to *the custom of trade*, and the *common law*, are *money*, are *cash*, and *not securities* for *money*: Nor, did the merchants, and bankers of Hamburgh ever enter into any consideration of coins, or any estimate of the usual amount of current money. They knew, before

fore the Bank restriction began, that they could not, under the existing law, melt, or export the current coins: Did the Bank restriction, then, effect any thing more, than to lock up the gold coins, from the melters, and exporters? Did not the traders, and bankers of Hamburgh know this circumstance, that *the coins*, which before they could not export, or melt, were now locked up; that the Bank of England was thus, in some sort, transformed into the Bank of Amsterdam, which always receives, and never gives out, bullion. And are not all those questions answered, affirmatively, by the subsequent state of the exchanges, during the *thirteen* years of the Restriction, when they were favourable, in *nine* years, and unfavourable, only in *four*. This experience of *thirteen* years demonstrates, that the traders, and bankers of Hamburgh always made their exchanges upon the pound sterling, according to the usual course, and expected to be paid in *Bank notes*, which they knew to be *cash*, and not securities for money: The practice of the *Clearing-house*, where millions of bills are daily liquidated, without any enquiries about guineas, or bullion, or circulating medium, or any thing but *Bank notes*, which the receivers, and payers, there, recognize, by a happy intuition to be cash, throws disparagement upon the whole theory, which attributes motives, and management, to the merchants, and bankers of Hamburgh, which they plainly never thought of; as they

they knew, that the carrying of such a theory into practice would impede circulation, and would stop the whole machinery of commerce.

10. After all those considerations, with regard to this head of *Exchange*, it becomes proper to add the EVIDENCE, which was given to the Bullion Committee, for its information. (1.) As to the *par* of exchange, Mr. C. LYNE said; "Though there are "fixed *pars* of exchange, between Britain and "other countries, they are *not* in *the smallest degree* "attended to; nor, do they, in *any manner*, serve "as a guide, for *exchange operations*; which, "as he conceived, are solely governed, by a "greater, or smaller demand for Bills *." Mr. J. L. GREFFULHE said; the *par* of exchange is of *no interest* to the practical merchant; the convenience of commercial calculation does not require the establishment of a par of exchange †."—As to the question, how far the exchanges are *ruled* by the *balance* of *payments*, between countries, Mr. GREFFULHE added; "the exchanges are influenced, "by commercial causes only, except the payments "of Government;--I conceive the cause of the present state of the exchange to be entirely commercial, with the exception of the payments, "which Government have had occasion to make

* Minutes of Evidence, fol. Rep. 60. Bills of Exchange, as we see from Harris, are merely *merchandizes*.

† Ib. 68, 69.

"upon

"upon the Continent, in the shape of subsidies, "and for payment of troops; it is *the balance of* "*payments*, which affects the exchange*." Mr. Ab. GOLDSMID being asked, "Do you consider "*gold*, and *silver*, as the only regulators of ex- "change?" answered, "*NO*; I do not; I con- "sider the *imports* and *exports*, as the *regulators* "of *exchange* †." With regard to *the causes* of *the low* or *adverse* exchanges: Mr. C. LYNE said, "The exchanges with the Continent being against "England, while the balance of trade is in her "favour, is, in my opinion, satisfactorily accounted "for, by the following facts:—The favourable "balance being chiefly against South America, "from whence, it has not yet come back, and can- "not yet produce its effect, in the general balance "with other countries, which are creditors; by a "greater amount of import, from the Baltic, "France, &c. than the export thither; by a *great* "*difficulty*, and *hazard*, in carrying on *bill*, and "*bullion*, operations with the Continent; as also "from some parts of the Continent to others; "which require greater profits to cover the risks; "and therefore, causes an augmented depression, "in the exchanges, the expence being doubled; by

* Ib. 70, 71. And, to which, he might have added the paying of the interest of the public debts to foreigners, amounting to more than £.600,000. sterling.

† Ib. 93.

the

"the want of a concurrence of drawers, and consequent competition, which would enable the few individuals engaged, in those operations, to controll the exchanges, and keep them so much depressed to their own advantage: By the great export of specie, for the purposes of Government*." To the same point, the *anonymous* CONTINENTAL MERCHANT says; "that the Government bills on the Continent have frequently produced a greater effect on the exchange, than bills of individuals to an equal amount, though not always so†." J. L. GREFFULHE ascribes the fall of the exchange, between London and Hamburgh, to the commercial situation of this country with the Continent; to the imports, and to the payments of specie; the deficiency of the exports: Another principal cause, he adds, of the low rate of exchange, is to be ascribed to the stoppage of the American circuitous trade, by the restrictions imposed, in America, whereby other Americans have been prevented from carrying their cargoes to the Continent, which would have operated upon the exchange, in as great a measure, as an export from this country; the greater part of the returns of such American cargoes being sent to their credit to the British merchants‡: The Continental expenditure of Government has, no doubt, affected the ex-

* Ib. 61. He might have added, the *equilibrium* of *export* being prevented.

† Ib. 84. ‡ Ib. 65—68.

changes,

changes *. The anonymous Merchant concurred with Mr. Greffulhe, in saying that, "the stoppage "of the American trade to the European continent, "in a great degree aggravated the low state of the "exchanges; as nearly the whole American exports "to the European continent were remitted, by "bills, to this country †." The ANONYMOUS *continental* Merchant was asked, "To what causes do "you ascribe the present unfavourable exchange?" "The first great depreciation," said he, "took "place, when the French got possession of the "North of Germany; and passed some penal de-"crees against a communication with this country, "at the same time, that a sequestration was laid "upon all English goods, and property. Whilst "the payments, for English accounts were still to "be made, and the reimbursements to be taken on "this country; the communication, by letters being, "also, very difficult, and uncertain, rendered it not "easy to find middle men [Exchangers] as in the "usual times, to purchase, and to send such bills to "England, for returns; whilst no suit could be in-"stituted, in the Courts of Justice, there [in Ger-"many] against any person, who chose to resist "payment of a returned bill, or to dispute the cause "of re-exchange; whilst those causes depressed the "exchange, payments which were due to England, "only came round, at distant periods ‡." Being

* Id. † Ib. 78. ‡ Id.

asked,

asked, "How much of the unfavourable exchange "was to be attributed to the effect of the measures "taken by the Enemy, and how much to the "effect of *the Bank of England paper not being* "*convertible into cash?*" he answered, "I ascribe "the whole of the depreciation to have taken place, "originally, in consequence of the measures of the "enemy; and *its not having recovered*, to the cir-"cumstance of the paper of England, not being "exchangeable for *cash* *; [that is, the gold of England, being locked up, could not be exported; and the coins of England, not being exportable by law.] The same ANONYMOUS Merchant went on to assign other causes, for the adverse exchange, namely, the large shipments, from the Baltic, which were drawn for, and the bills negociated, immediately, on the shipments taking place, the continued difficulty of the correspondence with the Continent; the curtailed number of houses, who were willing, to undertake such operations, either by accepting bills, for English account, which might be drawn from the various parts, on the Continent, where shipments took place, or by accepting bills, that might be drawn, from this country, for goods shipped abroad; the length of time, which is required before [re-exported goods, from the Continent] can be converted into cash, from the circuitous routes, that they

* Ib. 79. The anonymous Merchant did not know, any more than the Committee, that *Bank notes* are *cash*, according to the settled law of the land.

they are obliged to take; the very large sums, which were paid to foreign ship-owners, which, in some instances, as on hemp, has amounted to nearly its prime cost, in Russia *; some merchants, on the Continent, do not make advances on property, consigned as heretofore; from the course of our export trade, the Continent is largely indebted to this country, and in a much greater proportion, than what they would be, if trade had been carried on, as heretofore †; while the goods imported from the Continent are drawn for, on the shipment, and for such of these as are exported to the American States, this country gives credit; and it takes eighteen months, to bring the payments round. The imports, from the Continent, during the last year, of Baltic produce, German linens, and other products of the Continent, have been unusually great ‡. Mr. J. L. GREFFULHE said, "Goods "imported by the British merchant are paid for, "immediately, while the returns, for exports are "slow, and cannot yet, for the last year, have pro-"duced their due effect upon the exchange; the "imports from the Baltic, in 1809, have been con-"siderably more, than double the amount of the

* Ib. 82.—84. Mr. Greffulhe concurs, in this; saying that the freight from the Baltic amounted to £.50. per-cent. of the first cost of the goods. Ib. 66.

† Ib. 83. ‡ Ib.

same

" same imports, in 1808 *. The imports of wines, " and brandies, [and he might have added *corn*] " from France, have been considerable, and no " merchandize exported from this country, in re- " turn †; from the north of Germany, there has " been an excess of imports, above the exports; to " Holland, the exports have exceeded the imports, " although the imports have been great; Holland, " and the Ems, have been the principal points, to " which the exports have gone §: Mr. W. C. " CHAMBERS said, that the Continent is, at present, " much indebted to England ‖: and, he added, " that for goods exported, from the Continent hither, " for which they have paid, when re-exported to " the Colonies, the merchants give credit, for 12, or " 18 months; and he deemed those happy, who " get payment so soon:" He, also, said, " very " little exchange business has been doing of late " years; and this is owing to our exclusion, from " many parts of the Continent, to which before we " had free access ¶."

11. Such

* Ib. 66. He said, the balance of payments may thus be against us, while the general exports exceed the imports; Returns may be delayed, not only for months, but for years. Ib. 71.

† Id. ‡ Ib. 67. § Id. ‖ Ib. 103.

¶ Ib. 101. Mr. Ab. Goldsmid concurred, in those representations. Ib. 94. The difficulties, and penal restrictions, have not only lessened the number of Exchangers, but also have

11. Such, then, are the informations, which were given, in substance, to the Bullion Committee, by *practical men*, who are supposed, however, to be sometimes contradictory, often vague, and upon the whole unsatisfactory to the Committee*. But, is there any doubt, whether the Berlin, and Milan decrees still exist? Is there any doubt, whether the *Continental system* was in full operation, during the year 1809? Is there any doubt, whether British debts, and credits, and goods, were confiscated, under that system; or whether British merchandize could be exported, in 1809, to the Continent, under that system, without confiscation, and forfeiture? Is there any doubt, whether that system be not now rigorously enforced? That there are no such doubts, all Europe has testified, without introducing the witnesses, whom the Committee called, examined, doubted, and disbelieved. Without relying on the informations of *practical men*, who will be believed by the world, the whole question of the exchanges has been already discussed upon the existence of the Continental system, and the revolutionary measures of force, and fraud, which were practised upon the British commerce, and people, under that system of violence, and perfidy.

doubled the expence of exchange operations, which have risen to 2 schellings, Flem. on the pound sterling, said the anonymous Continent Merchant, ib. 74; and he repeated, again, the want of middle-men, who formerly employed great capitals, in exchanges, but, from the increased difficulties, and dangers of such exchange operations, are now rarely to be met with. Ib. 82.

* Report, 8° Edit. 18—22.

perfidy. The question of the exchanges has, in the foregoing Considerations, been discussed, under various views; and it has been invariably seen, that the causes assigned were altogether adequate to produce the obvious effects of adverse exchanges, and high prices of gold, and silver, without assuming what cannot be proved; or, insisting on positions that cannot be maintained. It is not necessary to derive any aid, from the additional facts, that the magistracy of Hamburgh have formally prohibited all correspondence with British subjects; that the bankers of Hamburgh have written to their correspondents, in London, declining any further commercial intercourse, from a regard to their own property, and persons. Thus, then, are the Hamburgh exchanges completely extinguished, under the outrageous operation of the Continental system: and thus has the whole question been decided, by *positive institute*, against the doubts, and assumptions, subtilties and theories, of the Bullion Committee; as the Senate of Hamburgh has done, what an Act of Parliament must have done.

12. Yet, does the Committee rely on the feeble information of Sir Francis Baring, whose evidence is interwoven into the contexture of the Report: "Sir "Francis considered the two great circumstances, "which affect the exchange, in its present unfavour- "able state, *to be the restrictions upon trade, with* "*the Continent*, and the *increased circulation of* "*this*

" *this country*, in paper, as productive of the " scarcity of bullion: And, he instanced, as an " example of a contrary state of things, the *seven* " *years war*, and the American war, in which " there were the same remittances to the Continent, " for naval, and military expenditures; *yet, no want* " *of bullion was ever felt**." But, without considering that, in those wars, the *Continental system* did not exist, with its *contempt* for commerce, and its *terrorism* to traders, it may be said that, the memory of good Sir Francis failed him; and the Committee, by adopting into their Report his failure, also fail: In fact, there was such a scarcity of gold, and silver, in the fourth year of the seven years war, as to induce the Bank, to change the established mode of its issues: In fact, there was an *extraordinary drain* of *cash*, from the *Bank*, in the last year of the American war†. We have now seen, in evidence, the egregious failure of both: That Sir Francis should fail, in his recollection, at his time of

* Report, 8° Edit. 19.

† " There being, says Anderson, in his Deduction of Com- " merce, 413, *an unusual scarcity of gold, and silver*, at this " time, in England, partly occasioned, by *much money* being " *carried out* of the nation, on account of the *expensive wars*, " in Germany, and America, and partly, by the large demand " for the current service of the year 1759." [the total grants of that successful year, being £. 12,749,860 !] In the last year of the American war, owing to various causes, " there was an " *extraordinary drain* of *cash*, from *the Bank*, particularly, in " October 1783, when the *Bank cash* was *lower* [in amount] " than

of life, and amidst his variety of affairs, might be expected: But, that the Bullion Committee, with the *Lords'* Report, 1797, on the table, should have stated to Parliament such *fictions* for *facts*, is quite wonderful*. Sir Francis had already shown, in his pamphlet, 1797, as we have seen, that it is quite unnecessary to appoint a Committee of Enquiry, when it is known, in the City, that *six*, *seven*, and *eight* per cent. profit may be made, by *exporting bullion* †: And, Sir Francis had, also, delivered his experienced judgement, in 1797, upon the main question; "As, a retrograde motion, in public "credit, is productive of consequences, which are "incalculable; I am averse, from the Bank re-"assuming their payments, generally, *during the* "*war*, whilst there is a possibility of their being "obliged, to suspend them again ‡." Sir Francis, however, was induced, when he more recently gave his information to the Bullion Committee, *to palter with it in a double sense*; yet, nothing would have been left, *in a double sense*, had the Committee, finally, asked him, "Is it your judgement, under

"than even in the *week*, *preceding* the 26 February, 1797, "when the Bank restriction took place." Macpherson's Annals of Commerce, IV—34. But, *this fact* does not altogether rest on the authority of this well informed Annalist. It stands upon the records of Parliament!

* See Lords' Secret Com. Rep. 259.

† Observ. 49. ‡ Observ. 68 69—81.

"our

" our domestic circumstances, and *under the opera-* " *tions of the continental system*, that the Bank " Restriction should be removed, during such a " war, with such an enemy?" His answer must have been, " In 1797, I submitted my opinion to " the public, that under the then circumstances, it " ought not to be removed; I have always been of " the same opinion, that under the existing circum- " stances, at home, and abroad, it ought, by no " means, to be removed." We may now perceive, that the Committee, by not asking the main question, *with a view to all circumstances*, Sir Francis Baring was induced to declare *a fallacy* to the public: This sort of fallacy runs throughout the whole examinations: By pressing points, which go to support a system, and keeping the special circumstances of the enquiry out of sight, the Committee made intelligent men speak a language, which conveyed opinions, that they did not hold. In making this reply, it is far, from my intention, to retract any of those sentiments of respect, for the person, and consideration, for the opinions, of Sir Francis Baring, which I have invariably held.

13. Let us now examine, whether the Committee be more happy, in its next topick, of *the par* of *exchange**. Either the Committee did not know the meaning of the *par* of exchange; or, for the convenience of theory, the Committee substituted the word

* Report, 8° Edit. 22.

*currency*, for the word *coin*; and by changing the one word, for the other, the Committee seized the '*vantage ground* of argument. It is the result of the comparison of the *coins* of different countries, which constitutes the *par* of exchange, and not a comparison of the *currencies*; as *coins* may be *assayed*, but not *currencies*, which may be in *paper*. Sir Issac Newton assayed the several *coins* of the different European nations, in order to ascertain their relative values, or *par*; but he did not assay *currencies*. "Hence," says Harris, the great assayist, "the equality of silver, expressed by different denominations of *coins*, constitutes what is "usually called, the *par of exchange*, betwixt any "two countries *." We thus perceive, how the Committee fails, either in its knowledge, or its argument. The *par* of exchange, as we have seen, differs from the *course* of exchange, in this: The par shows what any other nation, or town, *ought to allow*, in exchange, the *par* being *certain*, and *fixed*, by the intrinsic values of the several *coins*, when estimated against each other: But, the *course*, only,

† Essay on Money and Coins 115: And, with him concurs every other writer on money, and exchanges. The judicious Magens had stated enough on this point, when he said; "In "calculations of *the par*, regard is had *only* to the *coined silver* "of the several countries; and not to the *accidental price* of "*bullion*; for, this is never long the same." Universal merchant, 78. Magens, necessarily, excluded, from his contemplation, all *currencies*.

shows

shows what the Exchangers *will allow*, in exchange, which is *uncertain*, and *contingent*: There is another difference, arising out of the practice, and convenience of trade, which constitutes the difference, between the *true*, and the *nominal* par of exchange*. Those experienced exchange-brokers, De Mattos, and Eliason, alluded to the same nominal exchange, when they informed the Lords' Committee, in 1797, that *the par* of exchange, with Hamburgh, was always calculated upon the Bank money, which is fixed, and the pound sterling, which is also fixed, and unchangeable; that the one, and the other, are fictitious; and that the present par had been the same, as long as they could remember. Whether, then, *the par* be calculated upon the several *coins*, or upon the *money of account*, the one, or the other must be fixed, and unchangeable. In fair discussion, therefore, it is absurd to suppose, that the *par* of exchange can be calculated upon the *currency* of a country, which may consist much more of securities for money, than money itself, and may be subject to change, and depreciation, according to the nature of the securities, whether good, or bad. After

* It was with an allusion to the *nominal par* of exchange, that Magens, in speaking of the different ways, among merchants, of negotiating bills of exchange said, "If a bill of "exchange is demanded on Hamburgh, the negotiation is "always meant to be on the *pound sterling*; and the question is, "how many schellings and pence, Flemish, are to be received, "abroad, for each pound sterling." Univers. Merch. 82.

reviewing

reviewing the various exchanges of different countries, and of Portugal, in particular, and computing the *par* upon the *currency*, the Committee comes, at length, to the end, for which this computation, and that review was made, of finding not so much some defect, in our *coins*, as some depreciation, or *debility*, in our *currency* *.

14. The Committee now diverges to a supposed principle, which is said to have been long settled, and generally understood, "that the difference of "exchange, resulting from the state of trade, and "payments, between two countries, is limited, by "the expence of conveying, and insuring the pre-"cious metals, from the one country to the other †." What the Committee calls a *principle*, is by our elder writers, on such subjects, denominated the *natural exchange*; and the natural exchange is said to consist, in the whole charge of sending the thing itself, to be transported. How cumbersome this was needs not be told. And, it was the inconvenience of the *Committee's principle*, the transporting of the thing itself, at whatever trouble, and expence, which introduced the *artificial* exchanges: And, hence originated *bills of exchange*, the *par* of exchange, and the *course* of exchange, which have no difficulty in them to any, except to those, who wander away, from merchandize, to metaphysics: The Committee now states, as *a truth*, by all ad-

* Report, 8° Ed. 25.

† Id.

mitted,

mitted, "That the real difference of exchange, re-"sulting from the state of trade, and payments, "never can fall lower, than the amount of such "expence of carriage, including the insurance *." What is this, but dragging us back to the *natural* exchanges, far from the *course* of *commerce*, and the *practice* of *merchants*: And, is that to be assumed, in fair discussion as a *truism* in trade, which is inconsistent with the nature of commerce, and is disproved, by the practice of merchants: Such logic may be allowed, in the schools, but such speculations will be reprobated on 'Change: this reprobation will not only take place among *practical men*; but, that principle of the Committee had been already disproved by *speculative men*: Taking the *par* of the *natural* exchange to be the amount of the *whole charges of conveyance*, as the Committee assert, What does the great Assay-master of the

* Report 8° ed. 25. But, Mr. Blake, a favourite writer, of the present times, *on exchanges*, disputes the above-mentioned *truth*; and, he assures us, p. 29, that in the period, from 1774 to 1795, the exchanges, between Hamburgh and London were *frequently* so *unfavourable* to London, *as far to exceed the expence of the transit of bullion*. If the Hamburgh exchanges of November 1760, November 1774, January 1782, of July and September 1783, be compared with the prices of bullion, it will be found, that the exchanges sometimes fell below the par to more than double the expence of transporting bullion to Hamburgh. Research, might, with a little trouble, find other statements to the same purpose, if it were of any importance to dispute, pertinaciously, about the truth of a theoretic point, which is so contrary to the practice of trade.

Mint

Mint say? "The *price* of *bills may be reduced below* "*par*; but, bullion can never be lower than the "established standard, the Mint being always open "to receive it at Mint-price*." The Bullion Committee examined the late *Abraham Goldsmid*, in this manner:—"In ordinary times, when our gold coin "is at its standard, can the exchange be depressed "lower, by the state of [the] balance of payments, "than what it costs, to transport specie, or bul-"lion?" Answ. "Sometimes one way, and some "times the other, over, and above [under] such "price."—"How much over and above [under] "such expence, do you conceive?" Answ. "I "have known it differ, as much as five per cent. "either way, [over, or under]."—"Can so great "a difference as five per cent. continue, for any "considerable time?" Answ. "I have known, from "one to five per cent. continue, for three, or four "years."

* Harris on Money, and Coins, p. 121. Magens, another great assayist, and calculator, as well as experienced merchant, who knew practice, as well as theory, writing between the years 1740 and 1750, says: "Since a good part of the silver and "gold from Spain and Portugal are the returns for goods, from "Germany, sent thither, they [the Germans] have not always "occasion, for taking it all in goods, from England; and so, in "course, part of the same bullion will often, from England, "find its way through Holland into Germany, and, naturally, "the exchange from London to Amsterdam, for most times, "*must be under par*, so as to afford the charges of sending over "bullion; and so, in reality, I observed it to have been, and "you see, by the above course of exchanges, it was, in 1729." Universal Merchant, 85.

" years."—How long did it ever continue so high " as five per cent.?" Answ. " I have known it five " per cent. but very seldom, and not for a long time " together."—We have thus, from the examination of Abraham Goldsmid proof of *the fact*, in opposition to the Committee's principle. And, from all those facts, circumstances, and authorities, we may infer, that the famous *dogma* of the Committee is not only reprobated by *practical men*, but by *speculative* men, and by *scientific* men, as well as, by the still more overpowering authorities of *fact*, and *experience:* Now, we thus perceive, that the Committee has not only failed, as *assayists*, but as *logicians*, as far as it assumes to outargue fact, and to defy experience.

15. We are, in this manner, conducted by the Committee, to enquire, whether the practice of business consists, wholly, in *the transport of bullion*, as it supposes? Has this supposed practice ever existed, since the invention of bills of exchange, which came in the stead of *bullion carriage*. Did such a practice exist recently, either before, or since the Bank restriction? The very book, which lay on the Committee-table, would have answered, negatively, that question*. The whole mines of South America would

* Blake on Exchanges, p. 25, says, " that a very small part " of the payment of an *unfavourable balance* is effected, by the " *transit* of *bullion*." We also learn, from the more scientific Harris,

would not suffice, to settle the vast balances of our general payments, during the various turns of so vast a trade, as ours, taking in to the acccount the paying of dividends, the demand for subsidies, the craving of our vast establishments abroad, both civil, and military. On the contrary, the evidence, which was given to the Committee, by the practical men, evinced, that bullion can only be furnished, in a small proportion; and can only go a little way, in restoring an adverse exchange, while other merchandize can be furnished, to any amount; and would even more effectually restore the fallen exchange, if the commercial communication, with the Continent, were not restrained, by the Continental system. If we argue, indeed, with Mr. Blake, that *a very small part of payments is effected*, by *the transit* of *bullion*, what, then, becomes of that other

Harris, Essay, 123, who, speaking of the payment of unfavourable balances, says, "there is no way of bringing the balance "even, but *by the exportation of goods*, or bullion." Then, what said the experienced Magens, "I will venture to maintain, "that as trade is now carried on, *the country coin* has the least "share, in moving the wheels; silver, and gold, as bullion do "more: and, I will ask, Whether it be not possible, to gain a "*balance of trade*, without receiving it, in bullion? whereto, I "I answer, Surely, it is, by importing more in foreign com-"modities, useful every where, than we want, by our exporting, "and selling them to other countries, we may gain a *better* "*balance* in trade, than by receiving bullion." Universal Merchant, part ii. 5. What is this, but a description of the general course of trade!

dogma

*dogma* of the Bullion Committee, that *bullion* regulates the *prices* of *exchange*, while *exchange* does *not regulate* the *prices* of *bullion?* The experience of Magens had already revealed to the world, what a slight variation of a few *grotes*, in the exchange, will send bullion, to and fro, between Amsterdam and London *. Does not, then, *exchange command bullion* to go to, and fro, between London and Amsterdam, or Hamburgh? If such, then, be the *supremacy* of *exchanges* must they not *regulate*, not only the *motions* of *bullion*, but the rise, and fall, of prices, if it remain stationary. Those questions were all answered, affirmatively, by the merchants, bankers, and brokers, before the Secret Committees of Parliament, in 1797, who all concurred, in the position, that exchange regulates bullion, but not bullion, exchange. By examining the commercial events, during the effluxion of *thirteen* years of prosperity, under the Bank restriction, I have already shown, that the facts, and reasonings of those *practical men* had been

* Univers. Merch. p. 84. referring to the *experience of merchants:* "To avoid, says Harris, the charge, trouble, and hazard "of transporting *bullion* backwards, and forwards, for the supplying of different occasions, the method of discharging debts, "by *bills of exchange*, was introduced: This was an excellent "invention; these bills being as subservient, in *foreign* commerce, as *coins* are, in home traffic; for, by shifting of debts, "and credits, from one place to another, they so far answer "all the purposes of money." Essay on Money and Coins 108.

converted

converted, by events, into experience *. Shall dogmatism, then, be now admitted to defy facts, to outface demonstration, and to scoff at the practice of business!

16. After all those discussions, with regard to exchanges, far from me be the wish of detaining the more gentle reader, with *minute calculations* of the true variations of exchange, with Hamburgh, during the prosperous year 1809. In my foregoing considerations, I have reasoned the question upon the *average* of 11½ per cent. during the whole year, which seemed to be the true rule of argumentation. The Committee, by a very different computation, has reasoned the fall of the exchanges, upon a continued depression "from 16 to 20 per cent. through-"out the year †." The Committee may possibly be right; but, the probability is, that the Committee is mistaken. The exchange with Hamburgh, in 1808, according to an average of the *whole year*, was somewhat favourable. In the subsequent year, the lowest point, to which it fell, was 28. 6. being only 15½ per cent. *below the par*; yet, *this depression only continued during three weeks together*. During the *lowest month* of the *lowest year*, 1809, the

* The Bullion Committee asked the late Abraham Goldsmid, "Do you consider gold, and silver, as the *only regulators* of "the exchange? NO, I do not," said he. The proper answer to such a question, by such a person had been; Who ever heard of gold, and silver, being the only regulators of the exchange?

† Report, 8° ed. 27.

the average rate of this exchange was 28. 9. being 14¾ per cent. below par; the average of the whole year 1809, was 29. 9½ being 11½ per cent. below par. Now, the average of the whole year, among just reasoners, is the true criterion, as the whole enquiry turns upon this year of adverse exchanges. The investigation of the Committee was carried on, through the months of March, April, and May, 1810; and it was concluded, by the presentation of its Report, on the 8th of June. Now; the average rate of exchange with Hamburgh, during March 1810, was 29. 2, being 13½ per cent. below par, the same during April, was 31, and during May, only 31, which nearly amounted to 8 per cent. below par. It was not, then, correct, to state the depression of the exchange with Hamburgh, during 1809, *as amounting from* 16 to 20 *per cent.* and still more incorrect, to state this amount of depression, as a continued depression, throughout that period. The average rate of exchange with Hamburgh, during April, and May 1810, being only eight per cent. below par, as we have just seen, this was only *one* per cent. below the expence of transporting bullion to Hamburgh. Abraham Goldsmid informed the Committee, (and he is supported by the fact) that, during ordinary times, when the Continental system did not overpower all trade, and all exchange, the exchange had fallen five per cent. below the whole expence of transporting bullion to the

the neighbouring Continent. The foregoing facts, then, evince the feebleness of the foundation, whereon the Committee thought fit to raise so weighty a superstructure, as a *new system*, arising out of *something defective in our own currency*.

6. From those considerations, the Committee naturally diverged to enquiries, with regard to the *balance* of our *exports*, and *imports*; the Committee observing on this head, "how entirely the present "depression of our exchange, with Europe, is re-"ferred, by many persons, to a *great excess* of our "imports, above our exports *." But, with submission, this is not the true state of the question, at issue, before the public. The merchants, bankers, and brokers, maintained before the Committee, *not* that there had been a *great excess* of imports above our exports; but, that there had been, in 1809, a most extraordinary import, from the North of Europe, in *foreign ships*; *whilst* the *goods*, and *credits*, of the *British* traders were prevented, by the force, and fraud, of the Continental system, *from reaching their destined ports:* Hence, arose a great deficiency of funds, to pay, for those imports; and hence, the necessity of drawing so many bills of exchange, from Hamburgh, to a vast amount, so as greatly to reduce the COURSE of exchange, to their loss: Thus, the merchants, and bankers, are led to

* Report, 8° ed. 28,

complain

complain, that their informations are not so stated, as to comprehend the *whole question:* And, they insist, from the rise of the Hamburgh exchange, early, in 1810; from 11½ in 1809, to 8 per cent. favourably in April, and May 1810, that had their whole goods, and credits, reached their destined ports, the exchange would have become so advantageous, as perhaps, to have reached that point *above* par, which would have turned the current of bullion, from Hamburgh to London, as it undoubtedly did in 1798. The merchants complain, that their credit is injured, by not representing the *whole truth,* with all its accompanying circumstances: The bankers complain, that they are wronged, in their affairs, by representing a *depreciation* of our *own currency,* while the real disorder arises, abroad, from the fraudulence, and force, of the Continental system. And those merchants, bankers, and brokers, consider such representations, when unsupported by facts, and unillustrated, by circumstances, as misrepresentations, which, it must be allowed, are equally injurious to private, and public credit, that every one, who wishes well to himself, or the state, has an interest to support.

7. Accurate enquiry will probably find, that the traders are more founded, in their before-mentioned complaints, than might be supposed, from the obscure views of an interesting subject, which the Committee

Committee has given*: And, this truth will appear, whether we consider the balance of payments, or the balance of trade, during the *five* years, ending with 1809, without again adverting to the apocryphal *par* of exchange, which the Committee re-assumes, in opposition to those great assayists, NEWTON, Magens, and Harris †. "Our *debt* to foreigners, "says the last, operates, in the same manner, as a "balance of trade against us, to the whole amount "of the dividends, owing to them, [and he might "have added the stock sold by them;] and "the same he subjoins, is true, as to all foreign "subsidies," and he might have subjoined, also, our public expenditure ‡. Those various payments cannot now be so easily liquidated, as formerly, during the commercial freedom of the imperial towns, and the existence of the bankers, and exchangers, in every commercial city. Yet, the Committee assumes it, as a fact, that there remained a large balance of payments, on the favourable balance of trade of the four previous years to 1809, quite sufficient to meet the extraordinary causes of the depression of the exchange, in 1809; and in the course of the enquiry, the Committee repeatedly press that notion on the merchants, who stated the balance of payments, as the leading, and most pow-

* Report, 8° ed. 28—32. † Id.

‡ Essay on Money, 125. Magens concurs in this. Sect. xxxi. Univers. Merch. 12—15.

erful

erful cause of depressing the exchange, though not the *sole* cause, as the Committee misconceive *. In order to justify the rejection of the informations, which were given, by the *practical men*, on this head, the Committee studiously place the *balance of trade*, according to the *real value* of the exports and imports, between Great Britain, and all the world, during the *five* years, ending with 1809, which they contrast, by adding a statement of the *official* value of the exports and imports of Britain with the European Continent, only, for the same five years: By thus contrasting *real* values, with *official* values, the Committee fails, as much as *accountants*, as it had already done, as *assayists*: But, the object was, to show *large balances* of the trade, in *favour* of Britain, with the European Continent, during those *five* years, in opposition to the documents, annexed to the Report itself, which evince a contrary fact †: For, according to the *real* value of the exports,

* Wedded to this notion, the Committee disregards the evidence of the merchants upon the point; and even sneers at Mr. Greffulhe, for maintaining that, the state of the balance of payments *alone* was sufficient, to account for any depression of the exchanges, however great. Report, 8° ed. 31—2.

† Appx. Rep. No. 75, and 76: The Committee, indeed avow [Rep. 8° ed. 29.] that they place little confidence in the deductions, made even from the improved document of the Inspector Generals: "It is defective, as Mr. Irving has himself "stated, inasmuch as, *it supplies no account of the sum drawn* "*by foreigners* (which is at the present moment peculiarly "large)

exports, between Britain and the neighbouring Continent, the real balance of trade was against Britain, in the years 1805, 1806, and 1807, while, in 1808, the balance, in favour of Britain, was *two* millions less, than that exhibited, in the Committee's statement; and, in 1809, the favourable balance was only one half of what the Committee exhibits: Neither, was it very consistent with business, nor to the practice of trade, to bring forward the favourable balance of 1809, to bear on the exchanges of the same year, which, according to the course of commerce, and the nature of things, as stated, by the *practical men*, can only bear on the subsequent exchange, of 1810: Thus, according to the Committee's own documents, stood the genuine balance of trade on our *European commerce*, in the four following years *;

"large) on *account of freight, due to them*, for the employment "of their shipping." Now, what does Mr. Irving himself really, say? "I consider the account objectionable, in some "respects; the values are calculated, at the prices, in this "market, of *course* the *imports include* the mercantile profits, "and *the freights inwards*; the exports are *exclusive* of *the* "*freights outwards*." See Mr. Irving's Evidence, 222, of the 8° edit. By thus stating Mr. Irving to have said the contrary of what he did say, the Committee has misled some able men.

* Appx. No. 75—76; being the castigated accounts of the Inspector General.

1805

| Years. | Exports: real value. | Imports: real value. | Balance in *favour* of Britain. | Balance *against* Britain. |
|---|---|---|---|---|
| | £. | £. | £. | £. |
| 1805 - | 20,435,940 | 21,744,762 | - - - | 1,308,822 |
| 1806 - | 17,547,243 | 17,855,524 | - - - | 308,281 |
| 1807 - | 15,420,514 | 17,442,755 | - - - | 2,022,241 |
| 1808 - | 13,983,123 | 8,905,099 | 5,078,024 | — |
| Total £. | 67,386,820 | 65,948,140 | 1,438,680 | 3,689,344 |

We now perceive, by deducting the *advesre* balance of £. 3,689,344 from the *favourable* balance of £. 5,078,024, according to the Committee's document, that the balance of trade, on our *European* commerce, on those *four* years, was only £. 1,438,680. Now; it will appear, on the contrary, that the expenditure of Government, on the neighbouring Continent, during the *same four years*, with the remittances to foreigners, on their funded property, amounted together to upwards of £. 15,000,000. The subjoined Statement will evince the truth of this striking fact:—

| | | |
|---|---|---|
| In 1805, the expenditure of Government, abroad, was upwards of - - | £. 3,000,000 | |
| The remittances, for the *dividends* of foreign Stockholders, | 680,000 | |
| | | 3,680,000 |
| In 1806, the expenditure of Government, abroad, was more than - - | £. 2,100,000 | |
| The remittances, for *foreign* dividends - - - | 680,000 | |
| | | 2,780,000 |
| Carried up - | | £. 6,460,000 |

| | | |
|---|---|---|
| Brought forward - | | £. 6,460,000 |
| In 1807, the expenditure of Government, abroad, was more than - - | £. 2,100,000 | |
| The remittances, for *foreign* dividends, full - - | 680,000 | |
| | | 3,180,000 |
| In 1808, the expenditure of Government, abroad, was upwards of - - | £. 5,500,000 | |
| The remittances for foreign dividends - - - | 677,700 | |
| The remittances to foreigners, for *stock sold* - - | 655,800 | |
| | | 6,833,500 |
| The total *remittance* of those four years, | | £. 16,473,500 |
| But, deduct the *favourable balance of trade*, with *Europe*, in those four years - - - - | | 1,438,680 |
| Hence, the *real* balance of payments, to be sent to Europe, in bullion, or *goods*, in *those four years* - - - - - - - | | £. 15,034,920 |

We now perceive, that instead of a balance of *payments*, in favour of Great Britain, in her account with Europe, on those four years, as the Committee miscalculate, there was, in fact, a balance of payments against Great Britain of *more* than *fifteen* million. Much of this vast balance must have been liquidated, by the proceeds of the balances due to Britain, from her Colonies, and from America: But, as it requires full *eighteen months*, to bring round the payments, from the Colonies, and America, part of that grand balance, in favour of Europe, must have remained, as a pressure,

pressure, upon the year 1809: And, in addition to what thus remained, unliquidated, on those four years, ending with 1808,

| | |
|---|---|
| In 1809, there was so large an expenditure of Government on the European Continent, &c. as - - - - - - - - | 8,035,230 |
| Remittances made, for foreign dividends - | 592,980 |
| Remittances made, for foreign stock sold out - | 1,040,000 |
| Hence, the total remittances to Europe, in that year, was - - - - - - | £.9,668,210 |

In 1809, the trade of Britain with Europe, stood thus:

| | | |
|---|---|---|
| Exports, according to the *real* value, | £.27,190,337 | |
| Imports, according to the same value, | 19,821,601 | |
| Balance, in favour of Britain - | | 7,368,736 |

Now; this balance of trade, in 1809, amounting to £.7,368,736, could not, we see, meet the much larger payments, amounting to £. 9,668,210, which were obviously requisite, for the public expenditure, and for stock sales, and dividends, in the same year: For, it appears, from the information of the *practical men*, that according to the accustomed course of trade, owing to the usual credits, and to the Continental system, that the favourable balance of trade could not be made, usefully, effectual, till the subsequent year, 1810: So that the payments, in 1809, with whatever remained unliquidated of the outstanding balances, in the four preceding years, also operated on the exchanges of 1809, with little relief, from the

the great exports of this prosperous year; and, this operation, when superadded to the various other adverse circumstances, which were plainly stated to the Committee, by the *practical men*, did produce a most extraordinary depression of the Hamburgh exchanges, in 1809, though not so great, as from 15 to 20 per cent. as the Committee report. The favourable balance of trade, in 1809, began to operate, as we have seen, in the Spring-time of 1810: Thus, the Hamburgh exchanges, which fluctuated, at the end of 1809, and in the beginning of 1810, from 28. 6 to 29. 6, *rose*, in March to 30, and in April to 31; it continued, at 31, throughout April, and May; and again rose, in June 1810, to 31 and to 31. 2: So that, the average of the Hamburgh exchange, during the first six months of 1810, was 29. 11$\frac{1}{3}$, which is 11 per cent. *below* the par. This examination, then, of the before-mentioned documents, and accounts, exchanges, and facts, evinces, that the genuine informations of the *practical men* were accurate, however the Committee may disdain their judgements.

8. The Bullion Committee, at length, came to *two conclusions*, on this topick of *exchange*; or rather *one demonstration*, out of *two* inferences. Here is the concluding paragraph of the Report, on this essential head of the Enquiry*: "From the "foregoing reasonings, relative to the state of the

* Rep. 8° ed. 34.

"exchanges,

"exchanges, if they are considered a part, your "Committee find it difficult to resist an inference, "that *a portion*, at least, of the great fall, which "the exchanges lately suffered, must have resulted, "not from the state of trade, but, from a *change* "in the *relative value* of *our domestic currency:* "But, when this deduction is joined, with that, "which your Committee have stated, respecting "the change, in the market price of gold, that in- "ference appears to be *demonstrated*." Those are certainly the weightiest conclusions, which were ever drawn, from such doubtful premisses; considering that, they aim a blow, not only at the *private* credit of every individual, but a stroke to the *public* credit of the nation: And, in such a nation as this, *private credit* is a great object with every one, and *public credit*, as it is one of the great resources of this commercial country, has always been deemed, by the Commons House of Parliament, as a worthy object of peculiar care. It was quite apparent, from the day, on which the newspapers began to retail the opinions, and the recommendation of the Committee, that the well-informed people of this animated nation would not submit to such opinions, and such a recommendation, which deteriorate private fortune, and weaken public securities: And, what were intelligent men required to believe? That the Hamburgh exchanges, in June last, were fallen to a point of depression, from

from 15 to 20 per cent. below the usual par, when every broker, and every baby, I was going to say, knew, that the exchange had risen to 11 per cent.; that the price of bullion regulates the exchanges, when every practical, and every scientific man, know, that the exchange regulates the price of bullion; that the *Bank notes* are only *securities* for *money*, *depreciated* securities; when the citizens of London, who are experienced, in the custom of trade, and the magistracy of the country, who are acquainted with the common law; all know, that *Bank notes* are CASH, and *not* securities for money. Such are the dogmas, which are to support that weighty inference, which has already deteriorated private property, and lessened public credit. But, when this deduction is joined to the change, in the market price of gold, that inference, in the opinion of the Committee, assumes the dignity of *demonstration*. The Committee, then, did not know what all the world knows, that *gold* is a commodity, which, like all merchandizes, rises, and falls, in its price, according to the supply, and demand, in the market. The Committee did not believe, what men of science had written, and men of business had said, that unfavourable exchanges make bullion dear, and favourable exchanges, cheap; and so, that gold rises in price, when exchanges are adverse, and falls in value, when the exchanges are favourable. Sixty years ago, Magens had shown how few grotes,

grotes, in the prices of exchange, would effect the transit of gold, between London and Amsterdam. Sir Francis Baring, in 1797, had proved, *by the rule of three,* that an unfavourable exchange of 7, or 6 per cent. would make bullion pass, from London, to Hamburgh: But, when there is an adverse exchange of 15, to 20 per cent. the Committee does not believe, that any one would export bullion, for such a profit, though gold coins be every day seized, on board of ships, in the act of transportation. Experience had shown the world, that during the dear years, and under the Bank restriction, the trade of this nation not only made the various payments of specie for corn, and subsidies to the Princes, and Potentates, of the Continent, but supported the exchanges, by its exports: Yet, cannot the Committee be persuaded, that the *export of goods* is the *true equilibrium* of the exchanges, and not the transit of bullion. The Committee see various agents, public, and private, in the open market, buying bullion, for the purposes of peace, as well as for the uses of war; yet, the high prices are attributed to any cause, rather than to the various competitions of many buyers, and few sellers. The Committee had no suspicion, it seems, that a Company existed, at Paris, under the Emperor's eye, for draining this country of its specie: and, the Committee, notwithstanding all those facts, and circumstances, attribute the *high prices* of gold, not to

revolutionary

revolutionary causes, abroad, but, to a depreciated currency, at home: and, to this opinion the Committee is wedded, with all the conviction of *demonstration*.

But, I have done, with this *head* of the *Exchanges*; having finished what I had to say, in my considerations, on this topick. I will only add, how little consistent with good sense, it is, to suppose *cash* to have *depreciated*, rather than *prices* to have *risen*, contrary to general experience; and contrary to what was understood, in the Parliament, 1797, after great enquiry. It is as little consistent, with good sense, to argue, not only without proof, but against proof, that the traders, and bankers, at Hamburgh, knowing the custom of our trade, and the adjudication of our law, which attributes to Bank notes all the *qualities* of *cash*, and the arrangements of our Parliament, with regard to the Bank restriction, would give, now, fewer schellings and grotes, for our *pound sterling*, than formerly; when, under different auspices,—

> "Instructed ships did sail to quick commerce,
> "By which remotest nations are ally'd;
> "Which makes one city of the universe,
> "Where some may gain, and all may be supply'd."

But, in the present case, this supply, and that gain, did not take place: Under the *Napoleon code*, the universe is no longer one city, whatever poets may

may sing; and under the *Continental system*, remotest nations are no more allied, whatever Committees may think, or Ex-secretaries may say.

## — II. —

### Of the PRICE of BULLION.

1. From considerations, with regard to the *course* of the *exchanges*, the transition is easy to the *prices* of bullion; because they are very intimately connected: Under the *same state* of *trade*, the *course* of exchange, the *price* of bullion, and the *export* of goods, are all *correlatives*, from the universal practice of the mercantile world*. The merchants, bankers, and brokers, who were examined,

* The very well informed Harris, when shewing "how the "*price* of *bullion* is *influenced*," said: "A demand for bills upon "a particular place, raises their prices, as in other cases; and "when these prices have got up to a certain degree *above* par, "the price of bullion will be also advanced above the standard "of the country: for, dearness of bills causes a *demand* for "bullion to be exported; and in proportion of the demand to "the supply in the market, the price of bullion will be raised: "—Again; by transporting bullion, the price of bills will be "lowered; and that, again, will gradually lower the price of "bullion, until the prices of each are again brought to a par." And he adds, "there is no other way of bringing the balance "even, but, by the exportation of GOODS, or *bullion*." Essay on Money, 121—3. This is the opinion of all speculative men, as well as experienced merchants.

mined, by the Secret Committees of Parliament, in 1797, gave it as their opinions, that the course of the exchange overrules the price of bullion; and the two very experienced exchange-brokers, De Mattos, and Eliason, showed the Lords the *very pivot*, upon which the export-price of bullion turns, as the exchange is favourable, or adverse *; and of course, the low, or high, price of bullion. To argue, then, against the universal practice of the mercantile world, against the opinions of such assayists, as Harris, and Magens, against the informations of all the merchants, bankers, and brokers, to Parliament, in 1797, against *the fact*, as it occurred, in 1797, and 1798, is *most absurd* in *fair discussion*.

2. Sir James Stuart, that most profound *political œconomist*, has with his usual acuteness, shown how perplexity, and confusion, have been introduced, by confounding ideas, which are quite different, in themselves: "The terms, *gold*, and "*silver*, *money* of *account*, *coin*, *bullion*, and *price*," says he, "are often made use of as *synonimous*, "although no things can be more different:" (1.) The terms *gold*, and *silver*, should convey to us, he goes on to explain, *no other idea*, than that of pure *physical substances*: (2.) That of *money of*

* In confirmation of that reasoning, Magens, the experienced Magens said, in 1753, "Merchants know, that a difference, in "the exchange of five, or six *grotes*, will make gold and "silver, go to, and fro, between London and Amsterdam." Univers. Merchant, 84.

*account*

*account* represents an *invariable scale*, for *measuring value*: (3.) *Coin* conveys the idea of the public authority, ascertaining the exact proportion of fine, and alloy, in a mixed metal; and the realizing in a determinate weight of it, the invariable scale of money, sometimes correctly, and sometimes incorrectly: (4.) *Bullion* carries the idea of certain determinate mixtures of the metals, commonly ascertained, by some public stamp; and drawing their value exactly, from the proportion of the fine metals, which they contain, the workmanship being considered, as of no value: (5.) *Price*, again, when considered, as consisting of *coin* is a more complex idea still, since in it [the *coin*] are comprehended the value of the metals, the authority of the stamp, for the currency; the actual value of the *coin*, as a manufacture, above the value of it, as a *metal*; the common, and universal equivalent of all things; "and "the mean value of the currency, of which *price* is "supposed to contain exact aliquot parts, when, "perhaps, it does not." But, he adds, "all these "*different ideas*, are commonly confounded, both in "speaking, and writing;" and from this arises the principal difficulties: And, if three, or four people be engaged, in conversation, upon *money*, he adds, every one using the same term, in a different acceptation, the confusion becomes inextricable: "In like manner," he continues, "when we speak of "*coin*, and of *bullion*, that of the two ought to be

"considered

"considered as the *most fixed*, which changes its "proportion of value the least, with *respect* to *all* "*commodities:* Were *prices* attached to grains of "silver and gold, *bullion* ought, in that case, to be "considered, as fixed; but, as they [the *prices*] "are more attached to the *denominations* of the "*coin*, the *coin* ought to be considered as *fixed* *.' From the foregoing expositions of this very able writer, the more judicious readers will be enabled to trace the *fallacy*, which runs through the Bullion Report, by considering bullion as the *measure* of *prices*, rather than *coins*, or *money* of account, or Bank *cash* that, by law, is identified with both *money* of account, and *coins*. The same judicious readers may see something of the same *confusion of tongues*, above mentioned, prevail, constantly, in other bullion examinations, wherein questions are asked, in *one sense*, of *bullion*, and *coins*, and the answer given, in a *different sense:* Take the example of the examination of the very well informed Mr. Chambers, who is reprehended, by Mr. Huskisson, though he was not wrong †: Mr. Chambers was asked:—Do you consider a *Bank of England note*, for one pound, under these present circumstances, as exchangeable in *gold*, for what it represents of that *metal?*—Answ. I do *not* conceive *gold* to be a fairer *standard*, for *Bank of England notes*, than

* Political Œconomy, book iii. ch. 5.

† Pamphlet, 21—2.

than *indigo*, or *broad cloth*. The same question was repeated; and, Mr. Chambers said, "If it "represents twenty shillings of that *metal*, at the "*coinage price*, it is not." All that while, *gold* was as much *merchandize*, as broad cloth, and no more a *measure*, than broad cloth: The *fallacy*, then, consisted, in confounding *gold* with the *coin*; and Mr. Chambers, like an intelligent man, tried to draw the Committee, from the *fallacy*, by saying; Yes; if the Bank note of twenty shillings represents twenty shillings of *gold*, at the *coinage price*: The whole commercial world will reprehend the Bullion Committee, for asking *such questions*, more than fifty years *after* the Court of King's Bench, with LORD MANSFIELD, for its Chief, had solemnly determined, upon consideration of all the cases, that *Bank notes* are *cash*; are not *securities* for *money*; but *cash*, as much as *guineas* themselves: The POPULAR VOICE, then, speaking the language of solid sense, with the support of the custom of trade, and of the decision of the King's Bench, will overrule the Bullion Committee, which is supported, by none of those decisive authorities: And, the popular voice is clear, that *bullion*, whether gold, or silver, is as much a *merchandize*, as *broad cloth*, or a *bull*; and of course, ought *not* to be the *measure* of *Bank notes*, which are as much *cash*, as *guineas themselves*.

3. "In this country, say the *text*, and its com-

"mentary

" mentary *, GOLD is itself the measure of all " exchangeable value, the scale to which all money " prices are referred: It is so, not only by the " usage, and commercial habits of the country, " but likewise, by operation of law, ever since the " Act of the 14th of his present Majesty [finally " rendered perpetual, by an Act of the 39th year of " the reign] disallowed a *legal tender*, in *silver coin*, " beyond the sum of £. 25."—But, those acts applied to gold *coin* of the mixt standard, which never varies, and not to gold *bullion*, which does vary, every day, as a saleable commodity, according to the scarcity, or plenty of it, in the market: Those Statutes did not repeal the *common law*, which has recognized *Bank notes* to be *cash*, and to be receivable, as *cash*. The merchants, who were examined, except the anonymous Continental Merchant, maintained, that gold *bullion* is not the measure of value; but, is itself measured, in its varying value, like other merchandize, by the money of account, which Sir James Stuart assures us, never varies: Yet; the Committee justified the said *fallacy*, by the modes of Hamburgh; by the manner of securing a fixed standard of value, for the great commercial payments of that town: At Hamburgh, it is said, " *silver* is not only the *measure* of all " exchangeable value, but is rendered an *invariable measure*, except, in so far as, the relative

* Report, 5. Mr. Huskisson's Pamphlet, 6.

" value

" value of silver itself varies, with the varying sup-" ply of that precious metal, from the mines:" Now; the well-known fact, as stated to Parliament, in 1797, is, that the *Banco*, or Bank money, is, invariably, both the money of account, and the measure of value; being founded on, and corresponding with, the Bank silver, which is uniformly deposited, at a standard fineness, and at the fixed rate of 27. 10 per marc fine: Hence, all payments, at Hamburgh, are made in Banco, and gold bullion, which varies, in its price, is measured, and purchased, by Banco, that is invariable, while *bullion* rises, and falls, with the market price: So, in this country, the *pound sterling* is both the money of account, and the measure of value, which, of course, is invariable; all payments are made, by the pound sterling, or money of account, which is *the King's lawful money*, at *common law*: Thus, the pound sterling, uniformly, corresponds with the standard value of the gold *coin*, but it cannot correspond with the price of gold *bullion*, which varies, according to the demand, and supply, in the London market, any more, than it can, with any other merchandize: Now; the Committee, by assuming, contrary to the common law, as well as the common practice, gold *bullion*, as the measure of value, endeavours to make both the *pound sterling*, and the *Bank notes*, to rise, and fall, in their values, just as gold *bullion* rises, and falls, in the market: In short, the

the above *fallacy* consists, in substituting the word *gold*, for the word *coin*, and the word *bullion*, for the word *money*; and thus confounding the nature of things, and the meaning both of language, and of law: Such, then, is this famous *fallacy*, by which the Committee would prove, that *Bank notes* are depreciated, in opposition to the examinations of the merchants, and to the common sense of mankind; and by the same fallacy, the Committee attempt to make out the depreciation of the *current money* of Holland: as gold *bullion* had risen, at Amsterdam, to 17½ per cent. above the standard par. Abraham Goldsmid, having stated the extraordinary rise, in the price of gold *bullion*, at Amsterdam, was asked by the Committee, "When *gold* "is above par, would you not say, when compared "with *guilders*, the currency of Holland, that *guilders* "are *depreciated?*" No; said he, I should *not*. Mr. Greffulhe was asked a similar question, "Is not "the great difference, in the price of *gold* above "its par, at Amsterdam owing to the *depreciation* "of the *guilder?*" To which he answered, "I conceive *not*; the price of gold, as compared to the "current guilder, which is the regular mode of "selling, at Amsterdam, has been considerably "higher, at former periods." The same mode of enquiry was applied to the money matters of Paris; as the rise, in the price of gold bullion had been shown, to be higher at Paris, than at Amsterdam, and

and London: But, of such *fallacies* enough, when brought forward to outface fact, and to outargue experience.

4. The experience of 1797, and 1798, evinced, that a favourable exchange of £.10 per cent. would induce a vast influx of bullion: Is it not fair to argue, then, that an unfavourable exchange of 11½ per cent., in 1809, would occasion, in the same manner, a vast export of bullion, at a high price? But, that evil of an unfavourable exchange of 11½ per cent. was aggravated, in 1809, by the well known difficulty of getting *goods* sent to the destined port, owing to the Continental system: Now, the *export* of *goods* to the place of exchanges is, by the commercial world, deemed the true *equilibrium* of the low exchanges, and the consequent *high prices* of *bullion*. There was another evil, which contributed greatly to cause the low exchanges of 1809, which the Committee did not sufficiently consider, as it was unable to state the public account of the whole payments abroad: Although the balance of trade, in 1809 was large; yet, it was not equal to the whole balance of adverse payments, by *two millions and a half*, as we have already seen.

5. May not a greater demand, for bullion, in the *home market*, for domestic manufacturers, have produced a rise in the price of bullion, both gold and silver, on the London Exchange? Yes: Certainly, if there was a greater demand, even supposing the same

same supply, the prices would be higher; and if the supply did not keep pace with the demand, the prices would be much higher. Now; it is a fact, that there was a greater quantity of gold, and silver, plate manufactured, in Great Britain, in the ten years ending with 1809, than in the *ten* years ending with 1797*. While the manufacture of plate thus

* There were assayed, in Goldsmith's Hall, London,

| | Gold: lbs. | oz. | dwts. | gr. | | Silver: lbs. | oz. | dwts. |
|---|---|---|---|---|---|---|---|---|
| In the 10 years ended with 1809 | 16,942. | 11. | 9. | 9. | — | 1,130,451. | 3. | 18. |
| In the 10 years ended with 1797 | 10,171. | 10. | 2. | 22. | — | 919,283. | 0. | 19. |

There was much more gold, and silver, manufactured, in London, during the years 1797, and 1796, than in 1789, and 1788; so were there much more gold, and silver plate manufactured, within London, in 1809 and 1808, than in 1800, and 1801; the two first years of the *last* period of *ten* years, than in the year of peace, 1802. We may thus mark the progress of manufacture, and of opulence, during those ten years, under the *Bank restriction*. There are other assay-offices, in England, as we may learn from an account in the Bullion Report. In Scotland, also, we may see the same appearances, though in a somewhat less proportion, of the progress, there, of industry, and wealth: For,

| | Gold: oz. | dwts. | gr. | | Silver: oz. | dwts. |
|---|---|---|---|---|---|---|
| in the first ten years, ending with 1797, there were manufactured, in Scotland - - - - | 220. | 6. | 4. | - - | 214. | 0. |
| In the last ten years, ending with 1809 - - - - | 279. | 15. | 11. | - | 502,260. | 13.21. |

The two last years, 1809, and 1808, we may remark, were far superior to the two first years, in both the periods: And, it

thus hold its progress, we may perceive, from the foregoing documents, that the prices of gold, and silver, ought to have been higher, in the market of London, in the years, 1808, and 1809, than in any two years of the *two* wars of 1793, and of 1803. And, from those documents, we may, also, perceive, the greater industry, reproduction of capital, and wealth of individuals, during the war of 1803, than during the war of 1793. From these facts, and circumstances, we may rather infer, that the price of bullion, both gold, and silver, rose in their prices, than that Bank notes depreciated.

4. If a public agent come into the market of London, whether to buy coin, corn, or cotton, his operations are immediately felt, by the sellers, who raise the prices, in proportion to his supposed purchases. During the years 1808, and 1809, we had our armies to supply with specie, in every quarter of the globe *. But, what must be the enhancement of the prices of bullion, if there be *two* public agents, in the same market, at the same time, one English, and one French? It is easy, then, to perceive, from those proofs, how much the prices of specie must have risen, when the demand was urgent, and the supply was small: It must be inferred,

it is curious to observe, from the public accounts, that the duties on plate correspond with the progress of the manufacture.

* See the Accounts in the Appx. of the Bullion Report.

ferred, therefore, that the assumption is false, which supposes, contrary to the fact, that the prices of bullion did not rise; but, that Bank notes became depreciated.

6. If such disadvantageous effects on the prices of bullion followed, of course, from the operations of a public agent, for the support of the State, what must be the necessary effects of the purchases of bullion, in our markets, for our malignant enemy. That the French government has not only spies, in our streets, but agents, in our markets, for buying, and exporting our bullion, both gold, and silver, is certain. The Berlin, and Milan decrees, are so notorious, as to require no vouchers, for their details, or objects! France continues under every system of her government, to obstruct the trade, and injure the credit of Great Britain, by the most injurious intrigues*. How the operations of such a Company

* In 1792, as we know, from Barerre's public Declaration, the Directory formed a conspiracy, for draining this country of specie: for this end, agents, in London, were authorized, to draw bills on the *Caisse D'Escompte*, for whatever sums, at whatever exchanges; investing the produce of such bills, in gold, and silver, which were to be transmitted to France, where *the value of the precious metals was to be raised*; to meet such remittances of foreign coins, or *molten* guineas. But, Robespierre, by destroying the ruling party, ruined their project. And, the wish of the French government, wherever it may be lodged, to undermine our *public credit*, and private commerce, continues equally active, and more sly. The able, and eloquent *Letter*

Company upon the bullion market, both in raising the price, and exporting the commodity, need not be told. The ascertainment of the existence of such a Company, for such an object, as the draining this country of its gold, and silver, leaves the Bullion report, as it solves the Committee's scruples, without the value, or the weight of a straw: For, who would deliver the treasure of the Bank of England into such impure hands, for promoting so malign a project?

7. Arising from the same malignant policy, there is another cause, which operates powerfully, both in raising the prices of bullion, at home, and in transporting it abroad. The foreign shipmasters of 700,000 tons of shipping, as they know, that neither their property, nor their persons would be safe, if they were to carry merchandizes, from this country, to their own, employ brokers to buy up for them, at any rate, bullion of whatever kind, which they

*Letter on the Genius and Dispositions of French Government*, labours this important point. And, I will add a fact, which has been ascertained to me, by two persons, from foreign parts, who chose not to be named, any more than the *Continental merchant*, that a Company has been recently established, at Paris, under the all-powerful protection of the Emperor, whose sole object is, *to drain England of bullion*. A ship, which has been, lately, seized, carrying out bullion, in large quantities, conveyed with it several letters, which were intercepted; and which contained intimations, and traces, of such a Company, existing, at Paris.

transport,

transport, in various ways, and shapes*. That policy, then, operates, disadvantageously, in two respects; it prevents the export of goods, which would yield benefit to the shipmaster; and it drains us of our bullion, while it raises the price of the remainder. But, the evil does not so much consist, in employing foreign ships, in our transport, during the operations of war, as they always have, and ever must be; but, in the revolutionary measures on the neighbouring Continent, which prevent the foreign shipmasters, from benefiting themselves, and us, by carrying out merchandizes, rather than money: And the defect in the reasonings, both of Mr. Huskisson, and the Bullion Committee, consists, in constantly keeping out of sight, the *revolutionary measures*, before-mentioned, the *great causes* of the *apparent effects:* While this sort of sophistry continues so fashionable among our *political œconomists*, I will repeat a thousand times, that amidst *unfavourable* exchanges, it is the *export of goods*, which forms the *equilibrium*, the *corrective*, the *anodyne*, of those effects, and that cause: But, if there can be no carriage of goods to the proper market, owing to those revolutionary measures; then, can there be no *equilibrium*, *cor-*

*If we estimate the freight of 700,000 tons of foreign shipping, at £. 5. per ton, this would prove, that those shipmasters carried away in 1809, £. 3,500,000. sterling. The freights of foreign ships, from the Baltic, only, in 1809, was calculated to me, by an eminent Russia merchant, at £. 4,000,000.

*rective*,

*rective*, or *anodyne*; and there must, as cause and effect, be *the export* of bullion, if any be, and the *high prices* of that *commodity*, if any yet remain, in the home market*.

8. By such sophists, it is said, that upon the *recent reform* of the *gold coins*, the prices of bullion, immediately fell, as the necessary consequence. This may be considered, as little better, than an assumption of the point to be proved. It has been already shown, that the exchanges, with Hamburgh, did not immediately rise, as Lord King, and others supposed: I will now show, that the prices of bullion began to fall, before the recoinage, and not after, as some suppose. This recoinage took place, in 1773, according to Mr. Huskisson, whose *principles* lead him to deal much in *generals*: According to the late Earl of Liverpool, the father of the measure, "the recoinage was carried on "from the year 1773 to 1777, inclusive †." But, on such a point, we must be still more minute: In fact, the gold recoinage began, in August 1773, and ended with 1777. The prices of foreign coins, and bars, during February 1770, appear by an average of both, to have been £. 4. 0. 6. During some months,

* The whole examinations of the Bullion Committee support what is said above of the *scarcity of bullion*, in the *home market*: The frequent seizure of ships, in recent times, with large quantities of gold on board, in the *act of transportation*, demonstrates the great drain of bullion, by foreign shipmasters.

† Printed Report, 4.

months, the price remained, with some fluctuations, upwards of £. 4. In October, November, and December, the prices fell to £. 3. 18. 10. In the last six months of the subsequent year, the prices again rose beyond £. 4. They soon after rose still higher: And, in January 1772, they stood at £. 4. 1. 3. which seem to have been the highest of those times, when the average exchange, with Hamburgh, was 32. 7¼: They continued till July of the same year, at £. 4. accompanied with *low* exchanges: And throughout the last six months of 1772, the prices fluctuated down to £. 3. 18. while the exchange rose to 33. 10½. In January, and February of 1773, the prices rose a little: But, in March, and April, the prices began to vibrate lower; in May, they fell a little; in June they fell still more, so as to be £. 3. 17. 9: This was the price, in August 1773, when the recoinage began; and so it continued till August 1774*. By thus

* The Hamburgh Exchanges stood, meantime, thus;

| | | | |
|---|---|---|---|
| The average of March | - 1773 | was | 34.11 |
| April | - 1773 | - | 34.9⅞ |
| May | - 1773 | - | 34.10⅝ |
| June | - 1773 | - | 34.9¾ |
| July | - 1773 | - | 34.10 |
| August | - 1773 | - | 34.8⅝ |
| September | 1773 | - | 34.8¼ |
| October | 1773 | - | 34.9 |
| November | 1773 | - | 34.8⅜ |
| December | 1773 | - | 34.9¼ |

The

thus taking those comparative views of the prices, with the exchanges, what do we see, but *the exchanges overruling* the prices, as the *practical men* say, and as the Bullion Committee deny; *while the recoinage* seems to have had no obvious effect. It is a very curious fact, that, in 1801, the last year of the late war, while the exports amounted to £.37,786,857. the balance of trade to £.4,991,300. the Bank issues to £.15,459,050. and the Hamburgh exchange was *below* par 6 $\frac{1}{5}$ per cent. the price of gold rose to £.4. 6. and of silver to 5/11 per ounce; now, this price of silver is exactly the same as that of 1809, and the price of gold was nearly as much: But, there occurred, in 1801, no public enquiries, as to the prices of either, nor, was the *current money* said to have lessened, in its *real value*. Upon all those views of the subject, can that *depreciation* be assumed, in argument, as a *truth*, which is plainly disproved, as a *fact*.

7. There is some reason, however, to suspect, that the gold refiners, whose very trade consists, in sorting, and selling of bullion, both gold, and silver, at all times make a slight difference, between the precious metals, which they have so much, in their contemplation, and current money, which cannot be

| | | |
|---|---|---|
| The average of 1773 | - | 34·8$\frac{3}{4}$ |
| The average of 1774 | - | 34·6$\frac{1}{2}$ |
| The average of 1779 | - | 34·3$\frac{3}{8}$ |
| The average of 1776 | - | 33·5$\frac{5}{8}$ |

be converted into plate, or sold, as merchandize*. The other classes of our industrious people prefer *paper money* to the precious metals; as it is more convenient, in the uses of trade, and in the facilities of life. The whole kingdom of Scotland prefers *Bank notes* to *golden guineas.* By another accurate person, it was stated, "that the *medium* price of "dollars, from 1765 to 1797, was 63¼ pence!" The English coins, he added, being better than dollars 7½ dwts. the value of the *coin* is full 2*d.* per ounce, above the *dollar*; and the silver coins being

* The late Mr. Garbet, an eminent refiner, at Birmingham, stated, in a Paper, which I have before me, "that in 40 years "[from 1758 to 1798] the price of gold, in the London market, "by *Bank notes*, had not varied so much as 5¼ per cent." "In "the same market, he added, that between 1783 and 1793, "silver had varied, in price, £. 19. 6. per cent.; between June "1792, and D° 1793, it had varied £. 9. 3. per cent.; and in "1797, it had varied £. 13. 6. 4. per cent." "In the market "of Hamburgh, he stated, that the price of gold ducats fluc-"tuated, every year, between 1792, and 1797, generally, from "4 to 5½ per cent. advance upon the standard price of 6 marcs "banco per ducat: But, the variation, between the 1st of July "and the 11th of November 1796, was 7½ per cent. Between "the years 1782 and 1796, the variation was 11½ per cent. in "ducats. And the variation of Frederick d'ors, at Hamburgh, "during the years 1793-4-5 was £. 7. 4. 11. per cent." Thus much, from Mr. Garbet, which corresponds with more recent notices, as to this obscure, but interesting topick. Whatever there may be, however, in the above intimations, Mr. Merle, the Banker, and *refiner*, stated to the Bullion Committee, that gold bullion had *not* risen, with the increase of Bank notes: and he added, "I do not think, *Bank notes have had any effect* "*on gold.* Minutes, 53.

current

current, at only 62 *d.* per ounce; the conclusion is obvious. The same conclusion will appear still more obvious, from the following Statement: The average prices of dollars, from 1765 to 1797, inclusive, was - - 5. 3¼. p.oz.

| | sh. ds. |
|---|---|
| average prices of dollars, from 1765 to 1797, inclusive, was - - | 5. 3¼. p.oz. |
| Add the difference, in the value of *dollars*, from English *coin* - - | 0. 2. |
| | 5. 5¼. p.oz*. |

It thus appears that, the English silver coin being current, at 5/2 per oz. the average price of silver, from 1765 to 1797, was full 3¼ *d.* per ounce, above the current value of the silver coin. The average price of silver, in bars, from 1798 to 1809, inclusive, was - - - - 5. 7½. p.oz.;

Which is full 5½ *d.* per ounce above the current value of the coin. We have now before us the average price of silver, in the London market, for upwards of *forty* years, which was equal to 3½ *d.* per ounce, above the Mint price. Yes; says Mr. Muschet, all this, only, shows the *depreciation* of the *current money*, during *more* than *forty* years. Nay; did not those *popular* prices overrule the Mint? Well; in that period, the Mint did make some

* The average price of silver, in bars, from 1765 to 1797, inclusive, was a fraction above 5/4⅞, or nearly 5/5. per ounce, according to Castaign's Paper.

silver

silver coins; but, were they not, immediately, melted down, to bring the metal to those *popular* prices. What is this, but the *popular voice* over-ruling the *moneytary* system of the land. The popular voice has always overruled the moneytary system of every country. It did so, under the old government of France: It has done so, in Great Britain, since the well-known recoinage of K. William. And hence, arises *the folly* of buying silver at 5/5¼ per ounce, above the Mint price, to be coined, at a great public charge; and to be immediately melted, for *popular use*. It is, now demonstrated, I trust, that Mr. Muschet's *Mint price*, as a *standard*, is not an axiom of wisdom, but an axiom of folly! Now, as far as the Bullion Committee has been carried, by prejudice, to adopt Mr. Muschet's axiom, that Committee has recommended to Parliament a Mint policy, which had been condemned, for upwards of forty years, by the *popular voice*. And, "what are *axioms*, or principles more general, "according to the judicious HOOKER, but such as "this, that the *greater good* is to be *chosen before* "the *lesser*."

9. But, of all this enough, with regard to what I have to say, as to the *high prices* of *bullion!* It is apparent, that accurate reasoners must take an average of all those causes, before stated, of the dearness of bullion, in the London market, before they can form any opinion, either of the prices of bullion,

bullion, or of the state of our currency. (1.) It is the judgment of all those, who argue, from the practice of business, and from experience in traffick; who regard the *course* of *exchange*, the *price of bullion*, and *the export of goods*, in connection with both, as *correlatives*; that exchanges overrule prices; so that unfavourable exchanges, when they fall to a certain depression, will raise the price of bullion, even when goods are sent, as an *equilibrium*, and will raise the prices of bullion very high, when that equilibrium, as in 1809, cannot be applied. (2.) An augmented demand, for home manufactures of gold and silver, if the supplies of bullion be scanty, and uncertain, will raise the prices, in the London market, in proportion to the urgency of the demand, and the scantiness of the supply. (3.) If the public agents of opposing powers come into the bullion market, to buy up foreign coins, for the pay of contending armies, the competition of such agents, in addition to other demands, while no additional supplies arrive, must moreover enhance the prices of bullion. (4.) If in addition to those causes, foreign shipmasters, in great numbers, who dare not carry home merchandizes, transport bullion, this drain, by lessening the quantity, tends greatly to raise the prices, which were already high. (5.) If it be a fact, as is asserted by those, who know the fact, that there is a Commercial Company, at Paris, under the protection of the *Dominator* of

*Europe*,

*Europe*, for *the purpose* of *draining* this *country* of *bullion*, this fact alone would decide the practical question, at issue, Whether *bullion* be *dear*, or *Bank notes* be really depreciated.

10. I see, however, that the Committee doubt, notwithstanding the informations laid on its table, "whether, in point of fact, such a demand, for "gold, as is alleged, has operated, in the man-"ner supposed*." I cannot hope to convince the Committee: But, I will beg leave to submit some additional considerations to the view of those, who may honour this Tract with a perusal.

Here is the Committee's first position: "In the "sound, and *natural state* of the *British currency*, "the foundation of which is *gold*, no increased de-"mand for gold, from other parts of the world, how-"ever great, or from whatever causes arising, can have "the effect of producing here, for a considerable pe-"riod of time, a material rise in the market price of "gold*." Had the Committee said, in the sound, and natural state of the British trade, instead of the *British currency*, I should have regarded such a position, as a *truism*: For, according to the established practice of foreign trade, in its *natural state*, an abundant export of mercantile goods, as the proper equilibrium of the exchange, to the town, where the exchange is adverse, immediately raises up the exchange to *par*, and oftener so much above the par,

* Report, 8° ed. p. 5. † Ib. 4.

as

as to induce an influx of gold: This happened, in 1797, and 1798, as we have seen, after the Bank restriction; so as greatly to increase the abundance of gold, in the London market, and to reduce the price of silver, from 5/4½ per ounce, in 1796, to 5/2½, in 1797, and to 5/1, in 1798. But, is our foreign trade, now, in its *natural state?* The answer must be, that among sound enquirers, there is no propriety, no useful purpose, in arguing the question, at issue, before the public, on a different state of our trade, and currency, from the real one, which involves every one's fortune, and hazards the safety of the State.

The Committee now proceed to its second position, in the following terms *:—" If there were an " unusual demand, for gold, upon the Continent, " such as could influence its market price, in this " Country, it would of course influence, also, and " indeed in the first instance, its price in the Con- " tinental markets; and it was to be expected, that " those who ascribed the high price here to the " great demand abroad would have been prepared " to state, that there was a corresponding high " price abroad: Your Committee did not find, " that they grounded their inference upon any such " information; and so far as your Committee have " been enabled to ascertain, it does not appear, " that during the period, when the price of gold

* Ib. 5.

" bullion

"bullion was rising here, as valued, *in our paper* "[Bank notes] there was any correspondent rise in "the price of gold bullion, in the market [markets] "of the Continent, as valued, in their respective "currencies."

I will *first* proceed to point out a material errour, which runs through the whole reasonings of the Committee, on this topick, of the comparative prices of bullion, in Great Britain, and the neighbouring Continent, and particularly, in France;—I will, secondly, lay before the inquisitive reader, such informations, as I have been able to draw, from that Continent, for my own satisfaction. (1.) My objection to the Committee's reasonings on the *comparative prices of bullion, in Great Britain*, and the European Continent, arises from the well-known circumstance, that in Britain the *coinage* is made, at *the expence* of the public; so that every one, who carries gold bullion to the English Mint, receives back, free from expence, the same weight of coins: This practice of coinage, which, in every view, is very objectionable, has a necessary tendency to keep the value of bullion much beyond the relative value of bullion, on the Continent, where there is a *seigniorage*, and other charges, on the coinage, which, of course, bears down the value of the bullion, in proportion to such impositions on the mintage: Owing to those causes, bullion, in England, is always *dearer*, than it is in France; because the price

price of it, in England, is kept up by the Mint; while, in France, *bullion is allowed to fall* 8 *per cent. below the coin**. By not attending to those various circumstances, in the value of the bullion, where there is a *free*, and an *unfree*, mintage, the Committee, in its reasoning on this topick, has fallen into no less an errour, throughout, than 8 per cent.; so as to value the bullion of England too high, and the bullion of France too low, to that extent; an errour this, which Sir James Stuart would have taught any one to avoid: But, I have done; having neither time, nor inclination, to trace fallibility further, through a wilderness of misapprehensions, and mistakes, fallacies, and contradictions. (2.) I now proceed to the more agreeable task, of laying before the more inquisitive reader such informations, as I have, fortunately, obtained, from the Continent, with respect to this subject, in the convenient form of the queries sent over, and the answers returned †: (1.) Quer. Has there been any uncommon demand, at Hamburgh, during the last year, [1809,] for bullion? Answ. 1. The demand has been great; but, I

* For this very curious, and important subject, see the vastly sagacious Sir James Stuart's Political Œconomy, book iii. part ii. ch. 2. The best edition of this very interesting book, in the present circumstances of the dispute, between the Bullion Committee and the commercial world, is that of Cadell and Davies, 1805.

† The Answerers, of course, like the Continental Merchant, must be anonymous.

do

do not know, that it has been more so, than formerly? Answ. 2. Yes; on account of the contiguity, of Hamburgh, for the chief Northern trade of Europe, and the facility afforded by Lubec, in transporting specie to Russia, and the Prussian ports, and the interior navigation into Germany. Answ. 3. By a letter, from Hamburgh, dated the 24th of July 1810: "It appears, that there has been a "great demand, at Hamburgh, last year [1809] "for bullion; and it has continued more, or less, "from various causes; the contributions, payable "in France, are given, by some, as the chief cause; "while others consider the unusual large demand "for *ducats*, from Russia, occasioned by her wars, "with the Persians, and Turks, and the consequent "necessities of the Russian armies, at such a distance, from their immediate resources, as the "leading cause of the quantity of gold, and silver, "last year, being exported [from Hamburgh]; "silver was sent more to France, and gold to "Russia: Certain, however, it is, that the exportation to both countries, either direct, or by circuitous routes, was large beyond all other years: "Much gold was drawn, [from Hamburgh] by the "*Dutch*, for the purpose of coining ducats, which "all went to Russia: The large purchases of "wheat, in the Northern ports, and chiefly in Dantzic, since the early part of this year, occasioned "by the wants, on your side, have operated also

"on

" on the price of gold; the Poles being accustomed " to receive the amount of their corn, in Dutch " ducats, and always in a time of extraordinary de- " mand, carrying off to their own country a large " balance, in gold coin: Here are, therefore, inde- " pendant of many smaller, three good causes, for " the scarcity, at different times, felt, and for the " dearness of bullion. The price of gold has " varied, at different periods, very much, and been " at times very high."—The price of standard gold, calculated at the par of exchange with this country, upon Hamburgh, was, according to the latest quotation, from that city [in the summer 1810] 79⅛ per ounce: But, we must always recollect the before-mentioned reasoning of Sir James Stuart, which shows, that 8 per cent. must be added to such prices, for the *seigniorage* abroad. Quer. 2. Has there been any uncommon demand, at Paris, for bullion, during the last twelve months? Answ. 1. There has been lately an uncommon demand, at Paris, for bullion, both gold and silver; because, independently, of other causes, there has been a Company established, under the sanction of the Emperor, whose sole object is, to drain England of bullion, both gold, and silver, which are always, from 2½ to 5 per cent. higher, in Paris, than in Hamburgh, and Amsterdam. Answ. 2. There has been a great demand, for coin, owing, it is supposed, partly to the necessity of supply-

" ing

ing the armies, in Spain, with necessaries, which, owing to the poverty of the country, could not, as in the North, be made to subsist them; and partly, in consequence of the manufacture of bullion [in Paris:] It is understood, that an Association is established, at Paris, for the purpose of draining money, and bullion, from this country [Britain]; but, I cannot ascertain, if it be mere private speculation, or aided by Government; but, a *great deal is smuggled by every vessel*, not merely for the purpose of paying for their cargoes, and *freights*, but *on speculation for the purpose* of buying bills. France has no smaller paper currency than 50 francs, namely, about £. 20. 12*s*. sterling value; lesser sums are paid in coin; and specie is paid at the Bank, on presenting their bills, to any amount: France resumed her specie transactions early, in 1797. The consumption of bullion, at Paris, is very great; and it is supposed to be much greater than formerly; the present wealthy families, in France, having had no *legacies* of plate, jewels, or trinkets, need every thing, entirely new. Bullion has advanced at Paris, in about the same ratio as here: The present value of a guinea is equal to 22*s*. 6*d*. sterling, in that city.—I here beg leave to close this head of *informations*, as to the prices of bullion abroad, with desiring the more curious reader, to keep constantly in mind Sir James Stuart's rule, above-mentioned, on account of the

*seigniorage*

*seigniorage*, on the Mint, so as always to add 8 per cent. on the nominal prices, which are quoted; and so as, to correct this material error of the Committee. The *information* of the late ABRAHAM GOLDSMID concurs with those *transmissions* to me: Being asked, if the price of *gold* had fluctuated much at *Hamburgh*, during that period, he said; "Not much, not more than from 3 to 4 per cent. "it has not been more than 8½ or 8¾ per cent. "above par; nor, lower than 4 per cent. above "par; the par being 96." Being asked about the price of *silver*, at Hamburgh, he said: "The "price of bar silver, at Hamburgh, is always "fixed [at the bank]; yet there is a variation of the "price of silver [in the market], owing to the different demands there may be, from other countries, which require it."—Being asked the price of *gold*, at *Amsterdam*, as compared with the par; he said, "The price of *gold*, at *Amsterdam*, has "been as high as 17½ per cent. above the par, and "as low as 12½ per cent. above par, which it now "is:" Thus, have we seen above, that there was a *great*, and continued coinage of ducats, at *Amsterdam*, for Russia, and for Poland. Being asked about the price of gold, at Paris, he said; "That "a guinea is worth about 25*s*. and 44 guineas "would sell at Paris, for £.55. 12*s*. 6*d*.; and "upon the whole agreed, that the pound of gold, "in London, and at Paris, is at present, [March "1810]

" 1810] nearly of the same value, the difference " being only 7*s.* 6 *d.* per pound lower at Paris*." This goes to establish the truth of Sir James Stuart's theory, above-mentioned; and shows also, that neither Mr. Goldsmid, nor the Committee, were aware of that *theory*, which, after all this examination, proves, contrary to the Committee's notion, that gold was still higher, at *Paris*, than at London, 8 per cent. on account of the *seigniorage*; so that, in fact, the Committee deluded itself, by appearances, into an opinion, which, when embodied into the Report, cannot stand the test of criticism: What avails, then, the nicest calculation, when there is detected, in it, an errour of 8 per cent.!

11. The merchants, bankers, and brokers, who gave their informations to the Bullion Committee, referred the high prices of gold, in the London market, to three causes, chiefly: 1. The adverse state of the exchanges, which, necessarily, drained the home market; and which has been already shown to be a cause fully equal to the effect: (2.) The great demand, for exportation, not so much, perhaps, to satisfy a balance on the general account of payments, amounting in 1809, as we have seen, to full *two million and a half*, as to answer the various demands of the *mints*, and *manufactories*, and *military* matters of the Continent: (3.) The scarcity of bullion, in the London

* Com. Minutes, 8° ed. 116—17.

market,

market, to answer its demand, for domestic, and foreign, services. But, the Committee, while it *disbelieved* the assigned causes to be equal to the obvious effects, was quite unconscious, that there existed a cause, *the Company existing, at Paris*, for *draining this nation*, of its *gold*, which would have explained the various *phenomena*, that puzzled in mazes, and perplex'd with errour, the Commitee's enquiries.

12. In this sceptical state of the Committee's mind, it becomes necessary, to re-state the testimony which was submitted to its judgement. The very high price of bullion, at home, seems to evince some drain from abroad: In 1809, when the exchange was, as unfavourable, as 11 ½ per cent. the market price of gold bullion was £. 4. 6*s*. to £. 4. 8*s*. or 10 ½ to 13 per cent. above the Mint price, for gold, *which could not be exported*; and £. 4. 10*s*. to £. 4. 12*s*. being from 15 ½ to 18 per cent. above the current price for gold, *which could be exported*: This difference, between the prices of gold exportable, and gold not exportable, evinces a considerable demand, for exportation: And the Committee has reasoned, throughout, on the highest prices, without, however, admitting the export, in fact, or the demand for export *. (2.) It has, however, been proved before the Committee, that the price of transporting gold has risen to 7 per cent. which seems to imply, that

* Report 3.

much

much had been sent out. The chief object of this *great export* was said, by some of the informants, to be the demand, for the use of the French armies*. Mr. A. Ascher Goldsmid informed the Committee that, since the epoch of the Spanish war, Spanish *doubloons* have borne a greater price on the Continent †. He also disclosed, that the whole gold, which is sold, for home consumption, is less than a 20th part of the quantity, that is usually sold for export ‡. He added, that most of the late sales of gold had been made to *French* and *Dutch* merchants, for exportation §. Mr. Merle, the refiner, said, that "we have sold a greater quantity, for "exportation, during the last year, than formerly ||." —3. Yet, the Committee is not convinced of the reality of the rise of prices on the Continent: "So "far says the Committee, as it has been enabled to "ascertain, it does not appear that, during the period, "when the price of gold bullion was rising here,

* The Committee, however, observed, that if the demand *for the French armies*, had been lately much increased, "the "general supply of Europe has been augmented, by all that "quantity, which this great commercial country *has spared*, "in consequence of the substitution of *another medium* of cir-"culation." But, when that *other medium* came out of the Bank, did not the gold go into the Bank; whence, it has not been *spared* to the French armies, though particular perfons seem to be not quite unwilling, to spare to the French armies the gold retained in the Bank, by *approving the removal of the restriction.*

† Minutes, 56. ‡ Ib. 39.
§ Id. || Ib. 51.

"as

"as valued, in our paper [currency] there was any "corresponding rise, in the price of gold bullion, "in the market of the Continent, as valued, in their "currencies *!" When this was said, the Committee was not aware of the difference created, by the *seigniorage*, between the bullion, in the London market, and the bullion of Paris, as explained, by Sir James Stuart: The Committee did not advert to what A. Ascher Goldsmid, the gold-broker, said, that his house fixes the price of bullion, between the buyer and seller; and that, in fixing the price of bullion, here, reference is had to the prices, in the

* Report, 3: When the Committee reported the above opinion to the House; there lay before the Committee the subjoined Computations of the intelligent Mr. Greffulhe, on the 14th of March 1810; being A STATEMENT of the *value* of *Gold*, at Hamburgh, Amsterdam, and Paris, the foreign money being reduced into sterling.

| | | | Per Ounce: | | |
|---|---|---|---|---|---|
| At Hamburgh, - | Price 101 - | Exchange 29/ - | £.4 | 17 | 0 |
| At Amsterdam, - | Price 14¼ - | Exchange 31/6<br>Bank agio 1 p. cent. | 4 | 18 | 6 |
| At Paris, - - - | Price 105 - | Exchange 20/ - | 4 | 19 | 0 |

The prices of gold had been considerably higher, at those places, in 1808, and 1809, than the prices, upon which this Statement was made, in March 1810: For instance, at Hamburgh, in 1808 the price of gold fluctuated from 102, to 106; and from January to September 1809, the price of gold fluctuated, from 103 to 104¾. See Appendix to Report, N° 56. 58. and 60: At Amsterdam, the price of gold fluctuated, in 1808, from 10 to 17; and, in 1809, from 14½ to 20 above par. Ib. N° 56: So the above values of gold would be increased, in proportion to the higher prices in 1808, and 1809.

foreign

foreign market; and that generally the disposition of the market, here, concurs with the prices, abroad; because persons are willing to buy up to that price *, This regulation of the prices, here, by the rise, and fall, of the prices, abroad, might be expected, from the fact, which has been already mentioned, that nearly all the *gold*, which is sold, in London, is for export to the Continent, while the quantity sold, for domestic use, is not a *twentieth* part of that sold for export. Such facts, stated, by a broker, who knows them best, do not, however, shake the belief of the Committee, that it is the *depreciation* of the *money*, which regulates the price of bullion, and the rise, and fall of the exchanges: Neither did the information of Mr. Merle, the banker and refiner, much avail, when he informed the Committee, "that "the price of gold, in England, is rather less, than "it might be;" *considering the price on the Continent*; and he was positive, "that it is the pre-"sent high price on the Continent, which carries "gold abroad." Mr. Harman, the banker, concurred with Mr. Merle, in saying, that very high prices had been paid for gold, on the Continent, for particular purposes †; alluding, probably, to the great coinage of *Dutch ducats*, for Russia, and Poland. Mr. Greffulhe considered the fluctuations, in the price of gold, on the Continent, during the last two years, to have arisen from various

* Report, 55. † Ib. 144.

causes.

causes *. Mr. Whitmore, the Governor of the Bank, being asked his opinion, what had become of the greater part of our gold coin, which had disappeared, in the circulation, said, "that the high "price, abroad, had carried it out of this country †."

4. Come we now to the last cause assigned for the high prices of bullion, its *scarcity* compared with the demand, in the London market. The Committee has seen *no evidence* of any scarcity. Is not the general complaint of scarcity evidence of the truth of the thing complained of, as far as it is a declaration of the popular voice? Do not wars create scarcity of bullion, by the multiplied demands, for such an article? Did not the wars of 1756, and the American war, contrary to *the mis-*

* Report, 101.

† Ib. 121. But, the Committee, thereon, remarks, in the Report, that *he produced no proof of the fact*: Yet, is not the affirmation of the Governor of the Bank good evidence of such a fact; as he came there, as a *witness*, not as a *party*? Have not exporters of illicit gold been convicted of the fact, or rather of the crime? Have not the Custom-house Officers been occupied, daily, in seizing such gold, on board of ships, in the act of sailing? The *Sunday Observer*, of the 29th July 1810, has this paragraph: "A deposit of 9,000 guineas was, on "Thursday, discovered, in a snug recess, at the head of the "mast, of a small vessel, in the Thames, which had just discharged a cargo of *French wheat*; and another seizure of "4,500 guineas was made, at Deal, on the preceding day." But, is the *Sunday Observer admissible evidence*, the Committee asks? Yes; on such a point of *general notoriety*, as the export of guineas, in every foreign vessel.

*conception*

*conception* of the Committee, produce such a scarcity, and consequent runs upon the Bank? In superaddition to those causes, which are common to all wars, is there not a *malignity* in the *present war*, that peculiarly creates such a scarcity? And, whatever the Committee may disbelieve now, did not both Houses of Parliament, in December 1803, act upon the belief, that such a *malignity* would create such a scarcity of bullion, during the present hostilities, as would affect both private, and public credit; as would fasten upon the fortunes of every individual, and sap the foundations of the State; and was not the Bank restriction then continued, during the war, upon the belief of such a scarcity? After those general reasons, for believing that there did exist, in the London market, a *scarcity*, during 1809, let us hear what well-informed individuals say to the Committee.—Mr. Lyne, stated, "that in the course of "the last three years, there appears to have been "a great, and adverse difference, in the import of "bullion to this country, from foreign parts." A. Ascher Goldsmid said, "that a considerable "quantity of gold was formerly got from the Brazils, "through Lisbon; but gold is now sent over to the "Brazils;" and he added, "that this disadvantageous "change took place, in 1808, when the merchants, "trading to the Brazils, and Portugal, purchased "gold and silver bullion, [in London,] instead of "selling it, as before." These facts are confirmed by by the very well-informed Mr. Lyne, who is acquainted perfectly with the mercantile affairs of those countries. Mr. Merle, the refiner, and as such, well acquainted with such a subject, said, "Gold "is now, and has been very scarce; so that we "can hardly supply the trade; the want arising "from the *shortness* of the *supply*, and the *quantity* "*smuggled out*." Sir Francis Baring, having intimated to the Committee the scarcity of bullion, was asked, from what circumstances he inferred, there exists a *scarcity* of bullion? To which he answered, "From every information, that I have "ever received, or the opinion of any one person, "with whom I have conversed on the subject *." The inquisitive Mr. John Allan, who was in Spain, and Portugal, from 1802 to 1805, and again, in 1809, said, "that there is a scarcity of gold both "in Spain, and Portugal, but there was no want "of *silver*, in circulation: There was not so much "gold to be had, last year [1809], when I was, in "those countries, as there was in 1804 †." From the accounts of the American mines, which this peculiarly well-informed gentleman had obtained, with diligence, he stated, as the result of his enquiries, that, during the last half century, the quantity of *gold*, from all the mines of South America, has decreased, in the proportion of 6 to 5; and that the quantity of *silver*, during the same period,

* Minutes, 131. † Ib. 109.

had

had increased, in the proportion of 2 to $3\frac{1}{2}$ *. *Belief*, and *incredulity*, are like *taste*, about which, there can be no disputation. The twelve lawful men, who are usually summoned to settle facts, would find, upon the concurrent testimony of such intelligent, and respectable witnesses, when *speaking in their own art*, that there was a scarcity of bullion, in 1809. But, without entering further into this question of *belief*, and *incredulity*, it may be of more use, to show the more curious reader the *fallibility* of the Committee, on a most material point, concerning the true worth of different sorts of gold coins: The Report speaks, of the value of *Spanish gold*, as from $4\frac{1}{2}$ to $4\frac{3}{4}$ grains *better*, than *standard*; making about 4 *s.* per ounce *difference*, in value †: Whereas, Mr. A. Ascher Goldsmid, who is quoted upon the point, being asked, by the Committee, "What is the *fineness* of Spanish gold coin?" answered, "From $4\frac{1}{2}$ to $4\frac{3}{4}$ grains *worse*, than *standard*; making about 4 *s.* difference in value," [in every ounce ‡.] But, I have done! Enough has been said, and shown, to the more intelligent readers, for convincing them, that the Committee, as *assayists*, or *exchangers*, as *calculators*, or *transcribers*, are not quite *infallible*: When we see such *fallibilities*, in such men, is it not enough, to inculcate

* Ib. 108-9; and see his accounts in the Appx. to the Report. N° 21, to 28.

† Report 1.

‡ Minutes, 35. fol. ed.

inculcate on all men this *moral lesson*, that *moderate opinions* are most to be followed, as the *safest*, in *theory*, and the *best*, in *practice?*

## — III. —

### OF BANK NOTES.

We are thus led forward, by an easy transition, from the *prices* of *bullion*, at home, and abroad, to an enquiry, with regard to the *fancied depreciation* of *Bank notes*.

(1.) Neither any pamphleteer, nor any Committee, has yet *proved*, whatever they may have *inferred*, that the Bank notes have become, in fact, depreciated: It has, indeed, been said, that the great issue of the Bank paper, during late times, has produced unfavourable exchanges; that the unfavourable exchanges have raised the prices of bullion; and that the high prices of bullion, by a natural consequence, evinced a depreciation. Mr. Ricardo, by a pamphlet, inculcated such doctrines; Mr. Muschet, by tables of prices, and calculations of daily pars, has tried to strengthen those suppositions; and Mr. Blake, in the *title-page* of his pamphlet, on *Exchanges*, by speaking of "the *present depreciated state* of the currency," avowed his opinion, but disparaged his *own logic*, by taking for

granted

granted the very question, at issue. The Bullion Committee seems to have assembled, with the full conviction, that our paper money was then in a *depreciated state:* And the great effort of the enquiry was, to get the intelligent persons, who gave their informations, to say, that *bullion,* when bought with *Bank notes,* was higher, than when it was purchased with *gold coins:* This was attempted, after the effluxion of 13 years, the prosperous period of the *Bank restriction*; while the gold coins were locked up, by authority of Parliament, within the Bank: Yet, no one undertook to say, whatever might be wished, *that Bank notes had been sold, at a discount* *. We may thus perceive, then, that there is a sort of concert among *theorists,* in opposition to the practical men, to the common practice, and to the public good, for considering the paper money, the *Bank cash,* and even the *money of account,* as depreciated: But, the *fallacy* of their reasoning, I will not say sophistry, has been already shown, I trust.

2. None of those theorists, however, seem to have

* That experienced merchant, the late Sir Francis Baring, in his Pamphlet, 1797, p. 4. says: "If there were more *gold,* "than was wanted, confidence in it, as a representative sign, "would slacken, and it would no longer become a circulating "medium: If *Bank notes* were *augmented, so as to be sold at a* "*discount,* confidence would vanish, and those notes be no "longer a circulating medium." During the *late confusions,* in Ireland, *Bank of Ireland notes were sold there, at a discount.*

have been very studious to ascertain, from what *standard* the present currency, the *Bank notes,* and *pound sterling,* are thus supposed to have fallen. Some of them had learned, indeed, what Mr. Locke had said, in 1691, that an ounce of silver, whether in coin, or bullion, is, and eternally will be, of equal value to the same ounce of silver, under what stamp, or denomination, it might be in; whether it appeared in scarcity, or fulness, amidst the vibrations of demand and supply. Strange! that this position of Locke, which intelligent men had reprobated, should be again brought forward, as an axiom of truth, though it be only an axiom of fallacy. What a lapse was there, in the understanding of that philosopher! An ounce of silver always was, and ever will be, cheaper, or dearer, according as silver is plenty, and scarce: If many demanded Mr. Locke's ounce of silver, it would be dear; if few coveted the same ounce of silver, it would be cheap. Mr. Muschet, however, without considering much, perhaps, the fate of Locke's *fallacy,* in respect to his *ounce of silver* being the same, in every age, and under every circumstance, proposed as a substitute standard the *Mint price* of bullion: Mr. Muschet seems not to have adverted to the important fact, before mentioned, how much, and how often, the price of silver ha varied, in the preceding *forty* years, and had so seldom settled, at the *Mint price,* as to admit of coinage. *Gold,* also, in the same period, had often

often fluctuated, without much fixation: What sort of standard, then, is that, which continually shifts its value! He may suppose, perhaps, that 62*d.* worth of silver may form an *unit* of sufficient stableness to form a standard; or that the Mint price of *gold*, which is also subject to the vibrations of supply, and demand, may form something like fixation. But, the silver standard has been overruled, by the *popular voice*, which is the *genuine organ*, for announcing *universal price*: And, the *gold* standard has long verged to its final fate, from the same overruling cause: Thus, the same organ has already announced what the *gold prices* are, in the universal market; and how high they must continue to be, while revolutionary measures tyrannize over general trade. The price of gold, during the last forty years, has certainly been much more steady than that of silver; yet, enough of fluctuation, and much more unstableness, are now happening, from those revolutionary causes, to evince, that we cannot soon see the gold prices, at Mint standard; and, of course, the popular voice, announcing general price, to be much above the Mint price, will close the system of mintage, as to *gold*, as it has already done, for *silver*. When the Mint has performed all that can be done, in converting bullion into coin; yet, is *coin*, in the contemplation of mankind, but a *commodity*, which is subject, in the market, like other merchandizes, to the fluctuation of price, which daily arises from supply, and demand;

demand: Mr. Muschet, then, fails, in supposing the Mint price to be a standard, for measuring the value of Bank notes, as Mr. Locke had failed, in giving a standard, for fixing the price of silver bullion: When a recoinage took place, on Mr. Locke's principles, at a prodigious expence to the public, the people melted the new silver coins into bullion again: So, will the popular practice again, and again, put its own value upon gold bullion, from the prevailing notions of plenty, or scarcity, whatever Mr. Locke, or Mr. Muschet, can say, or the Bullion Committee can do: Practice will defy theory, and *experience* will overrule *speculations*, which, according to Shakspeare,

"Are to France the spies,—intelligent of our state."

(3.) Failing, then, in showing a *standard* of prices, which would, incidentally measure *depreciation*, or *enhancement*, all those theorists fail, spies as they may be, in showing the real *depreciation* of *Bank notes*. The popular voice says, that *bullion*, in fact, is *dear*: And, I have already shown a dozen distinct causes, for that effect; every one of which would produce dearness of bullion. The revolutionary measures, which I have indicated, consisting partly of force, and partly of fraud, have completely deranged, both the supply, and the demand, of the bullion market; and against fraud, and force, *theories*, and metaphysicks, are opposed, in vain. The same popular voice has declared, that there is

a *great*

a *great demand*, for Bank notes, from the multiplied uses of daily life: In fair discussion, then, is it not absurd, to argue, that Bank notes, which are greatly demanded, are greatly depreciated; since *demand*, and *depreciation*, are contradictory qualities! Now; upon all those grounds of fact, and experience, an appeal properly lies to the *popular voice*, from the "bookish theorick" of the Bullion Committee.

(4.) If neither the *ounce of silver*, nor the *pound of gold*, be proper standards of prices, because they fluctuate themselves, in their value, from the daily changes, which are effected, by supply, and demand, what is the standard? The answer must be, the *pound sterling* or *money unit*, which is recognized by law, though disdained by metaphysicks: The pound sterling is the King's lawful money; accounts are kept, in the pound sterling, with its divisions; debts are incurred, generally, though not always, in the pound sterling; the Courts of Justice enforce the payment of such debts, in pounds sterling, or lawful money, while Bank notes are recognized, by the course of trade, and the declarations of law, as *money*, as *cash*, full as much, as guineas themselves: Add to those considerations, that the whole exchanges of this commercial country are made upon the *pound sterling*, and not upon the golden guinea; and being thus made, upon the pound sterling, all foreign bills are payable, and have been paid, since the Bank restriction, in current

money.

money*. And Bank notes have, from the epoch of *the Bank*, been considered, by the Courts of Justice, in Westminster-hall, as money, as cash. Is it fair, then, is it fit, to say, in opposition to law, and in face of the fact, which is stated, by Sir Francis Baring, and in contempt of the table of exchanges, showing *nine* favourable years of exchange, against *four* unfavourable, that foreigners did not give the same number of schellings and grotes, in exchange, for the pound sterling, *since* the restriction as *before*.

(5.) Some observations have been put into my hands, by a commercial friend, which I will here interweave into my text, as they are acutely conceived, and ably reasoned.

1. "The nation, since 1797, has made no distinction between Bank notes, and gold coins, till now, that suspicion has been awakened, by the late

* The late Sir Francis Baring, writing on this subject, at the end of the year 1797, and speaking of what *foreigners* said upon this point, has this passage: "They were very much "astonished to find the *total amount* of *notes* to be so *small*, "compared with the commerce, and wealth, of the country; "and equally so, that after all, [the Bank restriction] *Bank* "*notes continued to circulate at par*." Add to this what I have already proved, that in the 13 years which have elapsed, since the Bank restriction [1797 to 1809] *nine* of those years have had *favourable* exchanges, and only *four* of them have been unfavourable. Moreover, has any one come forward to prove, that Bank notes have circulated otherwise, than at par? Does any one say, that Bank notes are not *money*, are not *cash*?

enquiries

enquiries of the Bullion Committee, who would persuade us, that Bank notes are not worth, within 15 per cent. of guineas; as a heavy guinea of standard weight [5 dwts. 9⅓ gr.] would sell [at £. 4. 12 *s.* per oz.] for 24*s.* 6 *d.* in Bank notes, if it were legal to sell it, as bullion, and that even a light guinea of 5 dwts. 7 gr. would sell for 24 shillings: But, it must be observed, that however high the price of *gold* may be, the *Bank note* only represents a guinea of the standard value of £. 3. 17. 10½. per oz.; and, therefore, it is unfair, in argument, to compare it with the bullion price; since, the guineas themselves, if in circulation, would only pass, for £. 3, 17. 10½. per oz.; and, it is, perhaps, better, that they should be hoarded, as by this means, they would remain in the country, though the holders lose the interest on them: while Bank notes, which are issued on undoubted security of 40 *s.* in the pound commercial property, are as good a circulating medium, and more convenient, for general payments. 2. Recollecting the recoinage of the *silver*, during K. William's reign, Mr. Huskisson reasons, throughout his pamphlet, as if we lived in K. William's times; having freedom of trade, and unrestricted intercourses, with the neighbouring Continent; whereas, for want of that unrestrained intercourse, which would take off our home manufactures, and Colonial products; and thereby raise the Hamburgh exchange, from 29. to 35, probably,

bly, we are thus prevented, from the chance of importing gold, [as in 1797, and 1798] or, which is the same thing in substance, from obtaining bills, at 35 exchange, which bring down the price of gold, at home, to the Mint price of £. 3. 17. 10½. per oz.; it being proved, in 1797, that while the Hamburgh exchange was under 33. 4; gold must go out of this country, and *vice versa*, when it was at 36. 6, gold, as certainly came into the country. But, in the present revolutionary state of the Continent, Bonaparte, robber like, is constantly exacting 40, or 50 per cent. *in specie*, throughout Germany, on all British manufactures, and Colonial products, or what he pleases: How, then, can it be otherwise, but that all the specie, either gold, or silver, that he can seize upon, should not go to France,—or that it should not be hoarded up, in Germany, to prevent his seizure of it, by whatever means? 3. If we were, then, required to pay in specie, while the exchange is 15 per cent. against us, it is a physical impossibility; it would be a sure way of *sending all the money out of the country*; and yet Mr. Huskisson tries to persuade us, that it would be the only way, *to bring it in:* Our comfort, however, is, that we can do as well without the *specie*, as with it; so long as we are certain, that the commercial property of the Bank is twice as much as the whole issue of Bank notes; and certainly, the more gold is hoarded, the more Bank notes will be wanted;

since

since gold hoarded is of no more use, as a circulating medium, than if it were not in existence. 4. Mr. Huskisson will have it, that gold, and silver, are the *only standards*, by which all *other articles* are to be *measured*. But, gold and silver, as gold and silver, are no more standards, or measures, than any other *goods* and *chattels*. Even when they are minted into gold *coin*, and silver coin, they are *not* the *only* standard, or measures. The money of account, and pound sterling, or in other words, the lawful money is the proper measure. And a paper currency might almost as well be established on the security of lead, tin, iron, or any other metal, or thing; provided there were a sufficient quantity of it to secure the holders of such a currency against any fluctuation of price, that might take place, in the articles, which composed the security: Solid bills of exchange, and Government securities, are as good guarantees, as any paper currency can rest upon; and such are the securities we have for the solidity of Bank notes: The country Bank notes, on the contrary, rest only upon the responsibility of the issuers; and great pains are taken, to force them into circulation: But, the Bank notes might be issued to twice the present extent, if they were not withheld, instead of forced, by the prudence, and discretion of the Directors. 5. Mr. Huskisson adverts to the state of Ireland, in 1803, when the exchange from Dublin to London was $17\frac{1}{2}$ per cent. while

while that of Belfast on London was only 7¼ per cent. and between Dublin and Belfast 9 per cent. The Dublin exchange, he says, was corrected, when the over-issue of the Dublin Bank notes was reduced; whereas, Mr. B—— assures me, that the issues of those notes never were reduced; but the high exchange was owing to the people about Dublin, during the rebellion, and for some time after, remitting their property to England, for safety, which eventually went back, and the exchange was then restored to its present level. I think it, however, very probable, that if the Dublin Bank notes were refused to be taken as cash, a part of them might, during the rebellion, be called in; and so would the Bank of England notes, if they bore an agio against guineas, in the general currency of people's payments.

(6.) Although Mr. Huskisson confidently maintains, that if *bullion* [coins], were in general circulation, every article would fall 20 per cent.; yet, this is more easily asserted than proved; two years ago, the exchange on Hamburgh was nearly at par, and there was no want of gold; and yet every thing was *then*, as dear as it is *now*; the gold in *bullion*, and the gold, in *specie*, being then of the same value, people had no motive, for hoarding up the guineas; but now, that the Bullion Committee has stated to the public, (and truly) that a guinea, at the coined price of £. 3. 17. 10½. per

oz.

oz. would, if allowed to be sold, as bullion, at £.4. 12*s*. per oz. fetch 24*s*. 8*d*. the holders of guineas naturally put this value of 24*s*. 8*d*. upon them, and withhold them, from circulation; but, notwithstanding this, our Bank notes are not regulated, by the advanced price of bullion, if it should even rise to £.10. per oz.; they only representing the guinea, at £.3. 17. 10½. or the Mint price; at which the public are not only willing to take them [the Bank notes] but are continually craving for more, than the Bank Directors are willing to issue.

(7.) Whatever, then, may be the fluctuations in the general vaue of gold, and silver, as bullion, there is no fluctuation, in the *money unit*, or pound sterling, which, as the pound sterling, and money unit, are neither *coins*, nor *commodities*, is not subject to change: The pound sterling, therefore, is the true standard of *prices* of both gold and silver, as well as of bread, and beef, whatever Mr. Huskisson may say, idly, of *bullion*: But, is there not such a circumstance as *the depreciation of money?* Yes; certainly; and I have, on a former occasion, treated, at some length, of *the depreciation of money*, of which vulgar history is full *. It was reserved, for the late Sir George Shuckburgh, to reduce this enigmatical subject to a sort of

* See the last edition of my *Estimate*, 333—36, for my account of the *depreciation* of money, which is only *another word*, for the rise in the prices of labour, necessaries, and land.

system.

system *. But, the true, and the Parliamentary language, is, that the prices of land, of labour, and of the physical necessary, rise, sometimes more, and sometimes less, in particular periods †. The value of money, then, does not depreciate; but prices rise: And, therefore, the pound sterling remains fixed, as a standard ought to be. Doth it not follow, from the foregoing facts, and circumstances, that, seeing the pound sterling, and the Bank note, are identified, in the law, and usage of the country, that the one is as stable, as the other.

(8.) If money, then, does not depreciate, and it is prices, which only rise; if the pound sterling be fixed, and the Bank note be as stable as it, by identification, can it be said, in fair discussion, that the

* See his Table of the *Appreciation* of Money, in the Royal Society Transactions, 1798, p. 176.

† See the several Reports of the Secret Committees of the two Houses of Parliament, in 1797. On the 30th of March 1797, Henry Thornton, Esq. Banker of London, was examined before the Lords' Committee, thus: " Q. Have you reason to " think, there has been a great increase, in the whole scale of " the public income and expenditure? A. Undoubtedly. Q. Has " not a similar increase taken place, in the scale of *private* " *expenditure*? A. If you include several years past, *it cer-* " *tainly has.* Q. Has there not been of late years, *a rise* in " the *price* of *provisions*, and of *labour*? A. Certainly. Q. Has " there not been a great extension, in the manufactures, and " commerce of the kingdom? A. Undoubtedly, &c. &c." The whole of the examination of Mr. H. Thornton is of great length, intelligence, and importance, which is the more interesting; as there was no cross-questioning, and he spoke what he knew.

operations

operations of the Bank enter *directly* into contact with prices, though they may *circuitously**. We may now perceive, that it is the plenty, or scarcity, and other circumstances of supply, and demand, which rule the prices, more than the plenty of money. Magens, who is recognized, by Doctor Adam Smith, as an experienced merchant and intelligent writer, has argued this interesting subject, with great knowledge of things, and men. He insists that, "it "is with *labourers*, as with *commodities*; the price "is governed by plenty, or scarcity, more than the "abundance of money: And we see, daily, he adds, "that the price of grain is not ruled by the plenty, "or scarcity, of gold, or silver, but, by its own "superabundance, or defect, where we raise more "than we can vend, or where we could vend more, "than we can raise: So, with labourers, we conclude, when they are scarce, they command their "wages; when plenty, the wages command them; "that is to say, they will work for less gold, and "silver, in one case, than in the other. Hence, it

* I have said, upon a different occasion, "that the Bank "paper promotes industry, commerce, and circulation; that "all these create wealth; that riches beget luxury; that luxury induces consumption; and consumption, by augmenting "the demand, necessarily tends to raise the prices of labour, "and commodities." See my Estimate, 428. It is, in this sense, that I mean to say, that the operations of the Bank may, *circuitously*, come into contact with prices: But, the operations of the Bank tend, also, to make us an enterprizing, commercial, money-making, and free-spending people.

"is evident, that gold, and silver, are as much "balanced, by the plenty, or scarcity, of other "things, as they are by gold, and silver; and upon "that balance depends the difference of prices *." If these representations of Magens be true, and every man, who is as observant, as he was, will find an echo to his opinions, in his own recollections; may we not infer, that the clamour, which we hear of Bank paper, and high prices, is more feigned, than felt; and is, merely, an outcry of our being an industrious and enterprizing, a commercial and opulent, a noble and generous people.

(9.) The converse of those conclusions is very well argued, by one of the most accurate of writers †. "Since the plenty of money, in a nation, which "has no mines of its own, is greater, or less, in "proportion to its trade with other nations; it may "be asked, whether to promote trade, and conse-"quently, to make a poor nation grow rich, money "may not be settled, at a low interest, by law, ac-"cording to the opinion of Sir Josiah Child, and "others? I answer, that this cannot be done, with-"out doing manifest injustice to all those, who "have their fortunes in money: Nor, need it be "done, if it be considered, that when a nation is "poor, all commodities, particularly provisions,

* Universal Merchant, 1753, xv—xvi.

† The late Doctor Byan Robinson, of Dublin, in his *Essay on Coins*, 1757, p. 20.

"and

"and land, are cheap, and labourers, and manufac-"turers, work for low wages; on which account, "persons, who borrow money, at high interest, to "carry on trade, will have that interest repaid, with "sufficient profit, when the commodities, which they "bought cheap, at home, are sold dear, in the "foreign markets of rich nations." When we compare together those accurate representations of Magens, and Robinson, may we not infer, from them, that if the object in question were, to obtain *low prices* of land, and labour, of provisions, and commodities, the adequate means must be, to impede the circulation, and oppress our commerce, to run down private credit, and thus undermine the public safety. With a slight deflection, from a people to projectors, we may say, with Dryden,

> " A party, *loving gold*, must rule this place,
> " Our temples ruin, and our rites deface."

(10.) We are, in this manner, conducted to an examination of the informations, which the *practical men* communicated to the Committee, with regard to the question, at issue, whether *Bank notes* be really depreciated: The late AB. GOLDSMID, who was first examined, in this enquiry, being asked pointedly, whether he thought *Bank paper* depreciated, answered explicitly, " I *never* considered " Bank notes, as depreciated *." Mr. W. C.

* Minutes of Evidence, 93.

CHAMBERS

CHAMBERS was asked, "Is it your opinion, that "the currency of England is depreciated?" answered, "*certainly not**." Mr. W. CUNNINGHAM was asked, "Do you consider the *paper currency* "of this country as depreciated?" answered, "I "*do not*:" Bank of *England notes* bear the same *premium*, as *guineas*, compared with Bank of Ireland notes †. Mr. Merle, the refiner, being asked, "If "he could not buy *gold* cheaper with *guineas*, than "with *Bank notes*," answered, "*NO*; that he "should pay the same price, in *guineas*, as in "*Bank paper* ‡." *Guineas* are only of greater value "if *melted*, and *exported*, contrary to law, to meet "the great demand, owing to the high price of "bullion, on the Continent §." Mr. C. LYNE said, "Bills, on foreign countries, are here obtained, "precisely, at the same rates of exchange, whether "they be paid for, in *Bank notes*, or in *guineas*; "and consequently, the remitter can place, by bill "remittances, as many florins, in Amsterdam, or as "many marks, in Hamburgh, with £. 1,000. in "*Bank notes*, as he can, with £. 1,000. in *guineas* ‖." Mr. J. L. GREFFULHE said, "In England, we "have no forced paper; no difference is made, in "favour of *specie*, in internal transactions; and the "*high price* of *bullion against Bank notes* is only "owing to the *demand*, for *exportation*; in pur-

* Minutes of Evidence, 102. † Ib. 130.
‡ Ib. 52. § Id. ‖ Ib. 61.

"chasing

" chasing a foreign bill, *guineas* will bear *no* superior " value to *Bank notes:* The high price of gold " should *not* be ascribed to *Bank notes*, but, alto- " gether to the *foreign* demand; the *dearness* of " *gold* cannot be called a *discount* on *Bank notes**." Mr. ABRAHAM GOLDSMID concurred with the very intelligent merchant, Mr. GREFFULHE, who was quite equal to the whole question, in saying, that " in payment of a *foreign bill*, *Bank notes*, and " *guineas*, are *the same*; the receiver takes them, " as the currency, and pays them away, as *the same*" [currency†.] Then came the last, but not least, Sir Francis Baring, who said, " The *paper* of the Bank " of England has stood firm, for above a century, " and flourishes, at this moment, with unabated " confidence: The power reposed in the Bank is " great; their paper is the *basis*, on which the best " interests of the country rests; it is the *seed*, which " serves to produce the whole of its commerce, its " finance, and its agricultural improvements‡." Happy! had Sir Francis known the *law* upon the point; as it would have supplied him with more adequate terms of definition, and panegyrick, than *paper*, than *basis*, than *seed*; and taught him never to call Bank notes, by such an expression, as *paper*, not even with POPE, " blessed paper money:" But, for both, definition, and panegyrick, we must refer to lord MANSFIELD, the illustrious Chief Justice

* Ib. 70—1. † Ib. 93. ‡ Ib. 132.

of

of England, who, after argument, and consideration, declared *Bank notes* not to be *paper*; not to be *goods*, not to be *securities*, not to be *documents* for *debts*, but *money* to *all intents*, but *cash*, as much as *guineas* *. And *Bank notes*, being thus, in contemplation of law, *money* to *all intents*; and being thus *cash*, as much as *guineas*, are of course, by operation of law, the *lawful money of the kingdom*, as much as the *pound sterling*: (2.) But, *Bank notes* were considered, under very different views, in the Bullion Committee: The *anonymous* merchant was the only examinant, by the Committee, who considering *bullion* [uncoined gold of the tower-mintage] as a *measure* of *merchandize*, regarded *Bank notes as depreciated* †; because the *market price* of *bullion had risen*: Upon the same principle, this anonymous person must have admitted, in argument, that the currencies of Hamburgh, of Holland, and of France, are, also, depreciated, since gold bullion has greatly risen above par, as we have seen, at Hamburgh, Amsterdam, and Paris: Mr. W. C. CHAMBERS, in answer to a question, which was suggested, by the conceit, of calling *bullion* a *standard*, made answer, "I do not conceive *gold* [uncoined gold, *at our mint*] to be a fairer standard, for Bank of England

* Burrow's Reports, i. 457.—*Cash*, says Dr. Johnson, is *money*: properly *ready* money; money, in the chest, or at hand. It is something *better*, than money, we may thus perceive.

† Minutes of Evidence, 76.

"notes,

"notes, than indigo, or broad cloth*:" The intelligent Mr. GREFFULHE concurred, in this way of thinking; saying, "the low exchange, in my opinion, "does not arise, from our receiving Bank notes, in "payment, for bills;—Were the circulation of this "country *confined to gold, and silver*, the export of "which being prevented, it would produce no "effect whatever on the rate of exchange, different, "from what it is, now, the payments being made, "in *Bank notes*†:" (3.) There is no difficulty, in this question, when *the terms, gold*, and *silver, money of account, coin, bullion*, and *price*, are properly *explained*, and *understood*, as I have already explained them, from Sir James Stuart s *political œconomy*‡: And, the doubt arises, only, when men, and writers, and reporters, use such terms, in *ambiguous senses*; so as to speak of *bullion*, of *gold*, and of *silver*, (uncoined at our mint) as *coins*, when they *are* NOT; of those *terms*, as measures, or standards, when they are *not*, or as any thing else, than merchandizes, as Mr. Chambers considered [uncoined gold] to be, *no more* a measure, or standard, than indigo, or broad cloth: If I could possibly conceive, that such speaking, writing, and reporting, thus ambiguous, and deceptive, were designedly intended, *to palter in a double sense*, with Parliament, and the public, on a question of so great interest to every one's fortune, I should say, that such *ambi-*

* Ib. 102. † Ib. 71. ‡ Book iii. ch. 5.

*guous*

*guous* language is not only *a fallacy*, but a DESPICABLE FALLACY.

## — IV. —

### Of the BANK AFFAIRS.

WE are thus led forward to some considerations, concerning *Bank affairs*, during late times. (1.) "It would be desirable," said the late Sir Francis Baring*, "for *the purpose* of *probing this question* "*to the bottom*, to ascertain what proportion the "issue of Bank notes has borne to the *gradual* "*increase of the commerce of the country*, although "the disclosure would not be prudent, in other "respects: But, I cannot think it possible, for the "one, to require an augmentation of the other, in "an equal degree; and it remains to be proved "that the amount of Bank notes, before the war "[of 1793] did *increase* in *proportion* to the *in-* "*creased trade* of the country, before the necessity "can be admitted, for an augmentation to the cir- "culating medium, in consequence of the large "additions to our trade, during the war, although "such additions is accidental, and temporary." This is certainly a very curious passage, written as it was, by such a person, at the end of the year

* In his *Observations on the Bank*, 1797, p. 4.

1797,

1797, some months *after* the epoch of the *Bank restriction:* It was certainly written, with great good intentions, and even with *simpleness,* compared with what we all know now of the vast, and permanent increase of our trade, and other important circumstances of our circulation. The grand disclosure of our Bank affairs was made, about the same time, by the Secret Committees of the two houses of Parliament: And what did that grand disclosure amount to? But, to tell the world that the Bank had a *surplus* of effects, beyond all claims, of £. 3,826,890. sterling money; exclusive of the debt, due from Government of £. 11,686,800; that is, that the Bank, after paying *twenty* shillings, in the *pound,* had a surplus of £. 15,513,690, good effects; that *the run upon* the *Bank,* was owing, as on former occasions of a similar kind, to the alarm of invasion; and that the only proceeding of the Bank directors, which could be construed into mismanagement, was that, during *the run,* they had *drawn in* their paper, instead of issuing it out: And, it should seem to me, that the Secret Committees rather inclined to lean to this last opinion. The commercial doubts of good Sir Francis may be cleared up, in the following manner: The three years, preceding the war of 1793, formed a period of prosperity, beyond all example; when the greatest export amounted to £. 24,905,200; when the largest issue of the Bank extended to £. 11,176,770: But,

But, in 1797, the value of exports had *risen* to £. 28,917,010; and the Bank issue had *fallen* to £. 10,403,000. We learn, moreover, from the intelligent Sir Francis, that *foreign* merchants were surprized, at the *smallness* of the *issue*, and at the *continuance* of the *Bank notes*, at *par*; not being aware, that the Bank, after paying 20 *s*. in the pound, had a clear surplus of £.15,500,000, sterling money; not being aware, perhaps, that Bank notes, according to *the course of trade*, and *the decisions* of law, are *money*, are *cash*, and *not securities*, for money.

(2.) In the true spirit of Sir Francis Baring, for *probing this question to the bottom*; for ascertaining what proportion the issue of the Bank notes has borne to the gradual increase of our commerce; I have formed a *comparative state* of *ten* columns, showing, *tablewise*, when, and upon what motives were issued the Bank notes, during the twenty years ending with 1809; whether those issues were made during peace, or war; whether amongst many, or few domestic enterprizes, which required much, or little capital; whether during a trade, increasing, or falling off; whether the exchanges were favourable, or adverse; whether bullion was plenty, or scarce *. From such a document, every reader, by an easy inspection, may satisfy himself, without applying to others, for information, whether the Directors, under all circumstances, acted fitly, or not, for the com-

* See the Appendix, N° II.

mon

mon benefit of the Bank, and the nation. This statement comprehends twenty years, the most eventful, in our commercial annals. It begins, with the three prosperous years, which preceded the bankruptcies of 1793, the epoch of the first French war. The first column exhibits four years of quiet, and sixteen years of warfare, the most malignant, in the diversified motives of hostility. The second column contains the number of Parliamentary provisions, in every year, for making the domestic improvements of our island, which have been carried on, with more activity, and success, during the struggles of war, than in any prior times of the profoundest peace; and as our struggles increased, our local improvements became more numerous, and more expensive. Connected with those domestic enterprizes, by which our island was *enlarged*, and meliorated, was the establishment of *country Banks*, district discounts, and reproductive capitals, while *the Bank*, by its accommodations, energized all those national objects. The three following columns represent the foreign commerce of the country, with the world, in its shipping, its exports, and its balance of trade; showing, by their gradual augmentations, that our foreign commerce, amidst the efforts of war, has more than doubled, in its advantages, and its gains; that the commercial capital of the traders increased, perhaps, in the same *ratio*, with the reduplications of their profits, and the attentiveness

attentiveness of their economy; while the discounts of the Bank gave to circulation facilities, and flow: But, while the Mint, as it was over-ruled by the popular values of silver and gold, coined but little; while the gold coin were retained in the Bank, by parliamentary direction; it is quite apparent, from the sixth column, that the Bank notes, which were issued, at the call of various demands, did not keep pace with the augmentation of our enterprizes, at home and abroad, and the flow of the circulation, throughout the land. During those twenty years of active trade, and vigorous hostilities, there appear, in the seventh column fifteen years of favourable exchanges, four of adverse, and one at par. The high prices of gold and silver, as represented, in the eighth column, evince, with clear conviction, the precariousness of the supply, and the constancy of the demand; as well as the important fact, that silver was rather higher priced, in 1801, than in 1809, and that gold was almost as high: And, we may thus, perceive the price of gold, by being so much higher, than the Mint price, during the last *ten* years, had also over-ruled the Mint; as the high prices of silver had already shown to all intelligent men, that the popular estimation of the values of the precious metals will ever restrain the theoretick principles, and usual practice of the Mint. This comparative state, [App. No. 2.] then, must appear to all intelligent readers, to be quite decisive of the whole question,

tion, at issue before the public: For, it shows clearly that, since the Bank restriction, in 1797, our *local improvements* had risen, in the *ratio* of 151 to 243; that our shipping outwards had risen from 1,500,052 tons to 2,230,902; that our exported cargoes had increased, in the *ratio*, of £. 28,917,010 to £. 50,301,763; and *yet*, the issues of *Bank notes*, excluding *post-bills*, which are out of the question, rose, only, in the *ratio*, from £. 10,403,000. to £. 18,015,700. deducting from this last sum the whole gold coins, that had been withdrawn from circulation; and the void being filled, by *country paper*; as the country banks encreased, in the mean-time, from 230, the numbers of 1797, to 700 and more, the numbers of 1809: And, it is thus quite apparent, that the *excessive issues* are not in the *Bank notes*; as the Committee suppose, but, in the country paper, as we have thus demonstrated.

(3.) In opposition, however, to thofe proofs, it is insinuated, by some, rather than said by others, that there is some laxity, in the management of the Bank: But, when we look into the *appendixes* of the two Reports of the Secret Committees, 1797, we may perceive that, the daily transactions of the Bank are duly recorded; that the vast details are constantly minuted, by the appropriate officers; and when Parliamentary Committees ask, for information, the most accurate accounts are readily given, from the Bank record, of the most extensive transactions of

its

its singular traffick: On this head, the Bullion Report, if we may judge, from the voluminous *appendix*, exhibits no want of documented information of every kind. Thofe documents, then, preclude the suspicion of relaxation, in the systematic management, which came down to the Bank directors, from their intelligent predecessors. The documents, which were before those Parliamentary Committees, evince a vigilance of observation, in the directors, both as to foreign, and domestic matters, that was felt, by the Chancellor of the Exchequer, and obviated by the agents of *foreign* powers *. Sir Francis, indeed, writing under the impression of 1797, talks of "paper "discounted, for *fictitious*, and stock-jobbing pur-"poses †." On the other hand, the Secret Com-

* See Mr. Boyd's printed Letter of the 9th of May 1794, to Mr. Pitt; in order to shew the minister of Finance that, the Emperor's Loan, as the borrowers might export goods, could not affect domestic circulation, or give jealousy to the Bank, This letter is very ably written, though somewhat tinctured, by the motive.

† His Observations, p. 8. At that epoch, there were two parties in the city; one said, that the Bank discounted *too much*; and the other, that they discounted *too little*. The Governor, and Deputy Governor have now avowed the real motives of their predecessors, in 1797. They considered the Bank, as a wealthy ship, in a violent storm: They deemed the safety of the ship, to be their first object; and all other considerations, to be merely secondary: They refused *discounts*, with deep regret: but, they acted, from the *necessity* of the occasion; and not from *ignorance* of the sad effects, both to trade, and the State. See the evidence of the Governor and Deputy Governor, in the Appendix to the Bullion Report.

mittee

mittee of the Commons, in their *first* Report of the 3d of March 1797, submitted to the House, "that "since the 25th of February last, considerable "issues had been made, in Bank notes, both upon "government securities, and *in discounting bills*, "the particulars of which could not immediately "be made up; but, as those issues appear to you "Committee to have been made, upon correspond-"ing securities, *taken with the usual care, and* "*attention*; the actual balance, in favour of the "Bank, did not appear to your Committee, to have "been thereby diminished*." We thus see, that the discounts of the Bank were made *upon security*, which had been taken, with the *usual care*, and *attention*, of the directors: We may observe, also, that the Secret Committee did not, on that occasion, consider the *mere amount* of *the issue*, as so formidable a point, as the Bullion Committee, without attending to our *existing circumstances*, declare it to be, contrary to fact, and experience; doing justice, however, to the *present directors*,—who have continued to conduct their business of discounts, and advances, according to the former *routine*; though without a sufficient watch over the *foreign exchanges*, and the *market price* of bullion; yet the fact is, that there is now, as there has always been, a committee of Treasury, at the Bank, for the very purpose of *watching exchanges*, and the market prices of gold

* Printed Report of the 3d March 1797.

and silver; neither is the Bank direction quite inattentive to the *great excess* of *country paper**.

(4.) The mere mode of issuing Bank notes, by discounts to individuals, and advances to government, seems to be disapproved, by the *Bullion* Committee, while the *Secret* Committee, 1797, did approve of that mode of issues, by discounts, and advances: The *Secret* Committee, seeing *the securities* to be taken, with the usual care of the directors, did not consider the mere amount of any deep consideration; while the *Bullion* Committee differs from the *Secret* Committee, on this point, and even disapproves of the directors conduct, to the full length of reprehension, while the directors acted, as their predecessors had done, under that approbation of the Secret Committee. Here, then, are clashing authorities! And, the question is, which of the two were right. The *Bullion* Committee was, plainly, mistaken, in supposing, that the Bank directors only take under their consideration, the *securities*, which are daily submitted to their consideration, for discount: The *Bullion* Committee are wrong, in supposing, that the directors have one point, only, within their contemplation, on such occasions: They have, constantly, *two* considerations, and sometimes more, before them; (1.) the *securities*; (2.) the *demands*; and (3.) another point of great moment, in this question, the *bound*, beyond which the Bank will not discount,

* Rep. 8° ed. 35—47. See my Appx. N° 3.

for

for any *one man*, or any *one house* of trade. They thus see before their intelligent eyes the *fitness* of the *security*, the amount demanded, by any one party, and the number of bills, which are daily offered for discount; and by intuition, full as much, as enquiry, they know the comparative extent of the passing, with the passed day; they have *a minute* of the daily discounts; and they have a record of their weekly issue; and from the two, they know, completely, the true state, both of the *demand*, and the *securities**. The solidity of the securities is a point of great consequence to the Bank, as a Company, which carry on discounts, for profit; but, the amount of the demand, whether it be great, or small, ardent, or weak, is a point of still greater importance to the people, as a commercial nation; because while the demand continues ardent, there can be no depreciation; since, in fair discussion, it is absurd to argue, that any thing can be, in the least, depreciated, which is greatly demanded, by many people; and on this topick, the *popular voice* will overrule the Bullion Committee: But, is it true, as we see it suggested, that the Bank does not take into its contemplation the daily vibrations,

* From long experience, saith Sir Francis Baring, the Directors of the Bank must understand, correctly, the amount to which their notes can circulate, without depreciation, or discount. Observations, 1797, p. 12.

in the exchange, in the prices of bullion, and in the other circumstances, which are connected with both? *NO:* The Bank has a wellknown *Committee of Treasury*, whose very business it is, to advert to the *course* of the exchanges, to the *prices* of bullion, to the import, and export of gold; to the buying, and selling of bullion; to *foreign loans*, and to domestic *Treasury accommodations.* All those points of vigilance, we may see, in full vigour, from the Reports of the Secret Committees, 1797. Upon all the foregoing grounds, the popular voice concurs with the Governors of the Bank, notwithstanding the Committee's intimation, of the immediate connection, between the Bank discounts, on the one hand, and the course of exchange, and the prices of bullion, on the other; so as to influence each the other, as cause, and effect.

(5.) Under all those limitations, it may be allowed, that the amount of Bank notes, in circulation, has greatly increased, since the epoch of 1797: But, have not the domestic enterprizes, the manufactures, the foreign trade, and general circulation, as well as the public revenue, doubled, and more than doubled, since the Bank restriction was adopted, by Parliament, into our policy, and law? Have not the gold coins been locked up to whatever amount? When we contemplate what has been thus abstracted, from circulation; and recollect what additional capitals were demanded, for our domestic improvements, and manufactures,

manufactures, for our home, and foreign trade, for the various, and augmented expenditures, private, and public; the average amount of Bank notes, at particular periods, are but small; and foreigners, as we learn, from Sir F. Baring, expected much more: Yet, small, as the whole issues appear, when compared with the vast capitals required; the discounts, and issues of the Bank, are of prodigious consequence, in giving flow, and facility to private capitals; and it is this facility, and that flow, which is commonly called *circulation**: Without the facility

* "Any thing may become a *circulating medium*, said Sir "Francis Baring; *paper* is as good a *representative sign* [circulating medium] as gold; and in many instances, it is better; "as it is more easily managed." Observ. 3. In p. 42, he adds, "Paper, as a circulating medium, is more than convenient; for, in those enlightened times, it is *necessary*, and "even *indispensable*." Sir Francis, however, never once mentions, throughout his whole book, that *Bank notes* are *money*, not *securities* for money, or a *sign* of *money*. Sir Francis sets out, p. 1, by saying, "*Circulation*, as the word implies, must "have a *pivot*, or a *center*, on which the whole can turn; and "that *center*, as far as relates to Great Britain, is the *Bank of* "*England*; whose notes *represent* that object [the center, I "suppose] for every beneficial purpose." It would have been fifty times more to the purpose, to have said, that *Bank notes* are *cash*, rather than that, they represent money: Well; Mr. Hume, the political philosopher, and Mr. Fox, the political orator, said, they never could understand *commercial circulation*. It may just be intimated to the followers of those great persons, that there was a folio book, published, at London, in 1650, entitled, *The Key of Wealth*, by William Potter, who treated the whole doctrine of circulation most systematically: I grant, Potter's *Key of Wealth* is a very rare book.

of

of discounts, the same capitals could not carry on such augmented commerce, nor sustain such mighty labours, as our local improvements: Nor, while the discounts continue to be made upon adequate security; while there is an urgent demand, for discounts, amidst additional undertakings, increasing labours, and augmented trade, the Bank notes cannot depreciate. There is a very accurate rule, for judging, when, and on what occasion, the daily issues of the Bank are too many, or too few: If there be a great demand for them, they are too few; if there be no demand for them, they are too many: If the circulation be saturated, then will it cast them out of the circle of commerce into the Bank: If Bank notes *regorge*, (to use an expression of Sir J. Stuart, the political economist,) in the hands of the holders, they will be immediately thrown back, from such hands, into the Bank. Upon the payment of the *dividends*, on settling for loans, and on other such occasions, we may perceive how fast the Bank notes are returned into the depository, whence they had just proceeded. But, from a view of all circumstances, it is apparent, that there cannot be a *legal* limit to the Bank issues; as the same limit would impede the circulation of the country; would bound its domestic enterprizes; and would cripple its foreign trade.

(6.) But, is any additional limit to those issues necessary, or requisite? The Secret Committee of the

the House of Commons, in its *first* Report, of the 3d March 1797, did not suppose such a limit to be requisite, and the whole Parliament, at that epoch, considered a *full*, and *flowing*, circulation, to be more advantageous to an industrious people, than a *scanty*, and *sluggish*, circulation. On other occasions, I have shown the *disadvantage*, and *danger*, of an *impeded circulation* to a commercial people: And, we have seen the House of Commons, acting upon that conviction, when it granted Exchequer bills, as an accommodation to traders, in 1793, and on every occasion, when Parliament has resolved, with true wisdom, to support public, and private credit.

(7.) While such a limit, by Statute, to the issue of Bank notes, is neither requisite, necessary, nor perhaps possible, it may be proper to enquire, if there be now, in circulation, *any excess* of *Bank notes*? The best answer, which can be given to this question is, an accurate Statement of the Gold Coinage, during the present reign; as we learn it, from the officers of the Mint:

| | |
|---|---|
| 1. From the beginning of this reign, in October 1760, to the end of 1772, there was coined, of *gold*, the amount of - | £. 8,819,390. |
| 2. The *recoinage*, from 1773 to 1777, inclusive, amounted to - - - - - | 19,591,833. |
| 3. The coinage of gold, from 1778 to 1796, inclusive - - - - - - | 28,863,437. |
| Carried forward | £. 57,274,660. |

Brought

| | |
|---|---|
| Brought forward | £. 57,274,660. |
| 4. The coinage of gold, from 1797 to 1809, inclusive - - - - - - | 8,940,114*. |
| The total, which was coined, in this reign | £. 66,214,774. |

If we suppose, that only one half of what was coined, from 1760, to 1796, inclusive, amounting to £. 57,274,660, continued to pass, from hand to hand, this amount would prove, that there remained, in circulation, merely, £. 28,637,330; or, in even numbers, £. 29,000,000. Well informed men have stated the amount of our gold, which continued, in circulation, at the epoch of the restriction, as about £. 30,000,000. Now; the bankers, traders, and brokers, who have been examined, by the Bullion Committee, agree, in stating, "that *gold* has almost *wholly disappeared*, from circulation."

| | |
|---|---|
| In the 11 years, from 1788 to 1799, the gold coined, amounted to - - - - - - - - - | £. 22,716,060, |
| In the 11 years, from 1799 to 1809, the gold coined amounted only to - - - - - | 3.972,312. |

This

* Of that last sum, nearly £. 5,000,000 were coined; viz. in 1797 - - - - - - £. 2,000,297. and, in 1798 - - - - - - 2,967,505.

£. 4,967,802.

The average of the subsequent years, from 1796, was indeed greatly reduced, as we might infer, from the *high prices* of bullion, which overruled the Mint.

This statement fully evinces a deficiency, in the *gold* coinage, during the last period, of £. 10,000,000; owing chiefly to the high price of bullion, which overruled the Mint. This deficiency could only be supplied, by Bank notes, and Country paper. The *increase* of Bank notes, during the 14 years, which elapsed, in 1809, was only £. 8,000,000, which consisted of £. 3,000,000, and upwards, in £. 5. notes; and the remainder, of about £. 5,000,000; of £. 2. and £. 1. notes *. In this view of the subject, can any one regard that augmented number of notes, both *great*, and *small*, as too excessive; taking into consideration, also, what is generally too much kept out of sight, the great increase of our domestic employments, the vast augmentation of our manufactures, and the prodigious addition to our foreign trade. The Committee, then, in speaking of the *excessive issue* of Bank notes, fail, egregiously, in the fact, whether the Mint accounts be considered, or the vastly augmented circulation be regarded, owing to our domestic

* From all the accounts, which have been laid before the Secret, and Bullion, Committees, it appears, that the increase of Bank notes of £. 5. and upwards, has not been great, *since* the *restriction*; the amount of 1795 being £. 11,000,000, and that of 1809 being £. 14,000,000; showing

| | |
|---|---|
| an increase of the *larger* notes of about - | £. 3,000,000; |
| and of the *small* notes of - - - - - | 5,000,000. |
| So that the whole augmentation is only - | £. 8,000,000. |

enterprizes,

enterprizes, our active manufactures, and our foreign trade.

(8.) The transition is easy, from Bank notes, to *Country-bank paper*. The epoch of banking is referred, in Anderson's Deduction of Commerce, to the year 1645, when the *goldsmiths* of London began to receive, and to pay, *cash*. Those goldsmiths' notes were the only *paper currency*, in Britain, from that epoch, till the Revolution. The goldsmiths may be deemed the first private Bankers. Till the rise of the Bank of England, paper currency was considered, as a thing uncommon; and as a *security* for money, rather than *money*. The Bank of England, which was established, in 1694, under an Act of Parliament, with a capital of £. 1,200,000, circulated Exchequer bills, on a stated allowance; issued Bank sealed bills, bearing an interest, which were soon laid aside; and sent out *Bank notes*, without interest, *payable on demand*. It is curious, as well as important to observe, that in the infancy of *Bank notes*, it was ruled, by Lord Chief Justice HOLT, that they were *money* *. It is said, by persons, who are otherwise well informed, that "the practice of issuing paper currency, within "the British dominions, first began, in Scotland," about the epoch of the Union: But, we have seen above, that the London goldsmiths' notes were the *first*

* Burrow's Reports, i. 458.

paper

paper currency, the *cash notes* of the Bank were the *second*; and these *last* were immediately recognized, by law, as *money*.

(9.) The epoch of the Bank of Scotland, which was founded on an Act of Parliament, was 1695, with a capital of $\frac{1}{12}$ of that of the Bank of England. The Scots Bank followed the steps of the former, though at a great distance behind. But, owing to the want of capital, and circulation, and commerce, in Scotland, thirty years elapsed, before the Bank derived much profit, from the country, or the country much benefit, from the Bank. At Edinburgh, however, were established, by the King's Charter, *The Royal Bank*, in 1727, and the *Linen Company*, in 1746: The Aberdeen Bank was set up, in 1746; and two Banks were founded, at Glasgow, in 1750. The Aberdeen Bank, and those Banks, at Glasgow, are the earliest *Country Banks*, that I have any where seen. There was some struggle, between the old Bank, and the new, in 1727, which brought some embarrassment on the business of Edinburgh; there was some competition, between the Glasgow Banks, and that of Aberdeen, which distressed themselves, and incommoded the country: But, real inconveniences first arose, in 1762, from issuing more paper, than the existing trade required, and from the artifices of individuals. But, some slight regulations of an Act of Parliament, with the prudent management

of

of the Chartered Banks, placed both the exchanges, and the paper currency of Scotland, in such a state of benefit, both to the Banks, and the individuals, as to be at once safe, and advantageous to a commercial people*: Beyond the accommodation of the *cash accounts*, which the Scotish Banks grant, banking cannot easily be carried, in its profits to the Banks, and its benefits to the country.

(10.) "The establishment of Country-banks, in "England, is of *modern date*, and *within my* "*recollection*, said Sir Francis Baring, in 1797. "During the interval, between the failure of the "Air Bank, in 1772, and the distress of 1793, "a very material change had taken place:—Banks, "he adds, had been established, in almost every "town, and even in villages, throughout the coun-"try; and, in the larger towns, rival establish-"ments were formed. Whilst their circulation

* 5 G. 3. ch. 49. See the informations of Mr. Mansfield to the Committee of the Irish Exchanges, 1804, for the salutary effects of that Statute; and the information of Mr. Gilchrist to the Bullion Committee, 1810, for the *sane state* of the whole system of the Scotish Banks. From their informations, we may infer, that banking, and Bank money, cannot easily be made more safe, or more commodious, to an industrious people. From Mr. Gilchrist we, moreover, learn, that there are, in Edinburgh, three chartered Banks, and two unchartered Banks, which issue notes; in Glasgow, a branch of the Royal Bank, and three others, which issue notes; and in other towns, one, or two and twenty, which issue notes: and all those Banks circulate notes to the amount of £. 2,500,000.

"was

"was thus greatly increased; and its beneficial "effects enjoyed, by the commerce, manufactures, "and agriculture of the country; their circulation "was founded on the *most insecure principle*, and "*liable* to the *most instantaneous convulsion*." Thus far, from the experienced Sir Francis Baring*; with whom I concur, in thinking that, the Country Banks, of England, like the Air Bank, may have promoted the agriculture, the manufactures, and the commerce of the country; while their establishments were founded on the most *insecure principle*, and were liable to fall, from any convulsion. We have just seen what happened to those Banks, in 1793. After that convulsion, there remained, of those Country Banks, only 230†. The same sort of Banks had again risen, in number, before 1808, to 600: and in 1809, to 721‡. We now perceive,

* Observations, 1797, p. 13—17. When I had this business before me, in 1794, it appeared to me, that of more than 400 Country Banks, which then existed, in England, 100 stopt; and all were shaken: Of the whole number, there were more than 279, whose notes were made payable, at the Bank, whence they were issued, or at some other Bank, or place, optionally. Estimate, 296—7. The Banks, at Exeter, as we learn from Sir Francis, and at other places, in the West of England, issued their notes, "payable *twenty days*, after sight, with interest, from the date." Observations, 18.

† Mr. Ellison's Evidence to the Lords' Committee, 87—8.

‡ Mr. Tritton's Evidence to the Bullion Committee: But from the whole number of 721, ought to be deducted the 21 unchartered

perceive, that the Country Banks of England, from a very obscure origin, within time of memory, have risen, from 320, in 1797, to 600, in 1808, and from this number, in 1808, to 700, in 1809, which circulate £. 20,000,000, at least, on very insecure foundations; and, at various epochs, have occasioned great convulsions, in our commercial policy. From the number, and unstableness of those Country Banks, many of them must become bankrupts, in every year; and, in proportion, to the number, and magnitude of such failures, must be the annual discredit of the paper circulation of this commercial country. Some persons of knowledge, and respectability, have mingled, in considering this subject,

unchartered Banks of Scotland, issuing notes, which Mr. Tritton, improperly, mixed with the Country Banks of England; improperly, I say; as the Banks of Scotland stand upon a different footing, and are governed, by very different principles: And Mr. Tritton, very probably, supposes, that there may be, in circulation, *twenty million* of the Country Bank paper. Mr. Richardson, however, whose business leads him to great knowledge of the Country Banks, assured the Committee, that the present numbers of the Country Banks were from 720 to 730; that in the two last years, 1808, and 1809, they had increased about 200; that he had heard the whole amount of their promissory notes, calculated at £. 30,000,000. And, he added, that owing to the vast augmentation of such promissory notes, the Bank of England notes are, at present, more confined to the circulation of the metropolis and its neighbourhood, than they were a few years ago. Report, 8° edit. 230—31. In this manner, then, were substituted promissory notes, or a *bad security* for money, in the room of *cash*; that is *bad money*, for *good money!*

ject, the whole paper circulation, in one vast chaos together; without considering that, the Bank of England notes, and the Bank notes of the country, are of quite different natures, and of very dissimilar stabilities. The Committee have thought proper to act, in this mannet; by treating of the whole mass of paper circulation, as pretty much the same, in value, and entirely the same, in depreciation; and by trying, to hang *the Banks* of the *country* upon the *Bank* of *the metropolis*.

(11.) In this view of an important subject, it is proper to enquire, in what light the Committee considered *Bank notes?* "The Committee speaks of "them, as *paper currency*; the Committee calls "them *paper*; *Bank paper*; *Country Bank paper*; "*Bank of England paper*:"—The Committee reports, as its opinion, "that there is, at present, *an* "*excess*, in the *paper circulation* of this country." If we look into the learned Commentary on this famous Report, by Mr. Huskisson, we may see our doubts cleared up*. "The Bank of England, says "he, as every body knows, is a chartered Company "of Merchants, whose *promisory notes*, for more "than a century, have constituted a very large pro- "portion of the *circulating credit* of this country: "From the institution of that Company, up to the "year 1797, there had been no interruption to the "*convertibility* of their *notes* into *money*." We

* His Pamphlet, 7.

now

now perceive this Commentator's opinion to be, that Bank notes are *promissory notes*, which, till 1797, were *convertible* into *money:* And, from this Commentary, we may infer, that the Bullion Committee did not regard *Bank notes, as money*, but only *promissory notes, convertible* into *money*. Now; is this a sound opinion; is it an opinion, consistent with the custom of trade; is it an opinion, according to the law of the land? The Chief Justice of England shall answer. On the 31st of January 1758, upon an action of Trover, for a *Bank note*, after hearing an ingenious argument, of Sir Richard Lloyd, and taking time to look into the cases cited, Lord *Mansfield* delivered the unanimous opinion of the Court:

"It has been very ingeniously argued, by Sir "Richard Lloyd, for the Defendant. But, the *whole* "*fallacy* of the argument turns upon comparing "*Bank notes* to what *they do not resemble*, and what "*they ought not* to be compared to, viz. to *goods*, "or to *securities*, or *documents for debts*. Now, "they are *not* goods, *nor* securities, *nor* documents "for debts: But, are treated as *money*, as *cash*, in "the ordinary course, and transaction of business, "by the general consent of mankind; which gives "them the *credit*, and *currency* of *money* to ALL "intents, and purposes. *They are as much money*, "as *guineas themselves are*, or any *other current* "*coin*, that is used in common payments, as *money*,

"or

" or *cash*. They pass by *a will*, which bequeaths " all the testator's *money*, or *cash*; and are *never* " considered as *securities*, for money, but as *money* " *itself*. Upon Lord Ailesbury's will [1748] £.900, " in *Bank notes*, were considered, as *cash*. On " payment of them, whenever a receipt is required, " the receipts are always given, as for *money*, *not*, " as for *securities*, or *notes*. So, on bankruptcies, " they cannot be followed, as identical, and distin- " guishable from money: But, are always consi- " dered as *money*, or *cash* *." Such, then, was the opinion of the Court of King's Bench: And, such has been the law of the land, since the epoch of the Bank, as explained by LORD MANSFIELD. Where, then, is the learning of the said Commentator; where, then, is the knowledge of the text itself! When Lord Mansfield, and the Court, took time to consider the cases cited, for the purpose of giving them a *better answer*, Lord Mansfield said, " He would not wish, to have it understood, *in the* " *City*, that the Court had any *doubt* about *the* " *point* †." Without the delicacy of LORD MANSFIELD, Mr. Huskisson is studious, by publishing his Commentary, in London, in Edinburgh, and in Dublin, to have it understood, in those cities, that he thinks, in opposition to the law of the land, that

* Burrow's Reports, i, 452—57: Lord Mansfield declared, that the Court were *all* of the same opinion; and that Mr. Justice Wilmot concurred.

† Id.

*Bank*

*Bank notes* are only *securities*; *depreciated securities*, for money. The Committee sat three months, to establish the same point, for the information of the City, the Court, and the Parliament, in opposition, equally, to the *law*, and the *circumspection* of Lord Mansfield.

(12.) As that great Judge showed *the fallacy* of Sir Richard Lloyd's ingenious argument; so may it be shown, with all the respect possible, indeed, *the fallacy* of that Committee, to consist, in several respects: (1.) The Committee does not advert, sufficiently, that we are engaged, in malignant warfare, with Bonaparte. (2.) It does not state, with adequate particularity, that British merchants cannot trade, within the limits of his influence; that British merchants cannot send goods to Hamburgh, nor can it be avowed, that they have any credits there; and of course cannot have any exchanges, but upon such disadvantageous terms; that the exchange with Hamburgh, and Amsterdam fell, in 1809, so low "as from 16 to 20 per cent, say the Committee; and being thus low, this revolutionary circumstance would alone, in the judgment of all bankers, merchants, and brokers, and as all experience evinces, drain this country of bullion. (3.) That in addition to this drain, the Committee does not advert, sufficiently, to the great, and constant demand, in the London market, for bullion, from abroad, and at home, during a scanty supply;

supply; so that bullion has risen, in price, beyond all calculation. (4) Under all those circumstances, the Bullion Committee supposes *the cash* to have depreciated, rather than *the* price of *bullion* to have risen: But, have not the prices of land, and labour, of necessaries and of merchandizes, risen greatly, during the last twenty years? Do not *prices* fluctuate more than *cash*: And, is it not, therefore, the most egregious fallacy, in the text, and its commentary, to argue, in opposition to all those circumstances, facts, and experience, that *cash* has *depreciated*, rather than, that *prices* have *risen*? The Secret Committees of both Houses of Parliament, in 1797, thought so, after examining the most intelligent witnesses, and weighing circumstances. (5.) But, that fallacy was committed, not only against law, but in opposition to the evidence before the Committee, and its Commentator *.

(13.) There is another fallacy, which runs through an essential part of the Committees Report: It confounds, in one general mass, the whole circulation of paper money, whether of the Bank of England, of the Banks of Scotland, or of the Country Banks of England. (1.) Nothing, as we have seen, has been imputed to the Directors of the Bank of England, as to laxity of management; as to the excess of their issues, considering the abstraction of the

* Report 93; Ib. 102; Ib. 128—30; Ib. 32: Burrow's Reports, 452, Hilary Term 31 G. ii. Miller v. Race.

gold,

gold coins, from the circulation, and the augmentation of discounts, arising from the more numerous enterprizes, at home, and the vast enlargement of our trade, abroad; and adverting, also, to the circumstance, that according to law, Bank notes are not *securities* for *money*, but *cash*, or money in hand. (2.) As to the Scotish Banks, it is quite evident, from the Statute, for reforming them, and from the evidence, which was given by Mr. Mansfield, in 1804, and by Mr. Gilchrist, in 1810; that their present management is perfectly safe; that their issues are fully within the demand of their circulation; that their principles are sound, and their practice most salutary. (3.) The Country Banks of England, which are obscure, in their originals, and doubtful, in their progress, which amount to 700 and more, and issue £. 20,000,000, and upwards, are undoubtedly too many, for permanence, and circulate too much, for security: They are an excrescence upon our commercial dealings of a dangerous tendency; but not a *superstructure* on the Bank of England, as the Committee say, without authority. (4.) If *superstructure* mean what is raised upon something else, there is little fitness, in saying, that they are *superstructed* on the Bank of England, which has always resisted their operations, and constantly denied them support. When a hundred Country Banks became bankrupts, in 1793, I remember it was commonly said, that the Bank, by

refusing

refusing to discount their bills, had contributed to their failures. Mr. Ellison, the Secretary of the Country Banks, informed the Lords' Committee, in 1797, "that he had traced, in his own mind, *the* "*distrust*, that had prevailed against the Country "Banks, in the first instance, to the Bank of Eng-"land's withholding its discounts, in the beginning "of the year 1793*." Mr. Richardson, more recently, has informed the Bullion Committee, that the discounts, which the Bank give to the Country Banks, or their connections, are but very scanty, and uncertain†. Now; it is neither good logick, nor sound law, to assert that, a structure has been raised on any one's land, when the owner has successfully resisted the builder. In this view of the subject, it is not easy to perceive any privity, any connection, far less any engagement, between the Bank, and the Country Banks, whatever the Committee may say of *the structure* of *the Country Banks upon the Town Bank*, or of the convertibility of Country Bank notes into Bank of England paper, or the limitation of the Country Bank circulation, by the amount of the Bank circulation, which are all assumptions, that are contradicted, by fact, by experience, and by law. (5.) It should seem, from the mode of examining the *informants*, that the Com-

* Lords Committee, Report, 89.

† Bullion Report, 8° edit. 179-80.

mittee imposes upon itself, in respect to this important topick: Mr. Richardson was asked, as to the *discounts*, by Country Bankers, whether they existed, before the Bank restriction? He answered, *Yes:* Were they practised, before that epoch, to a *similar extent?* *No,* he answered. What was the cause of *such difference* [of the greater extent of Country Bank discounts, since that epoch] Mr. Richardson answered; "I believe it to be, on ac-" count of the *increase* of the Country paper, and "*also of the Bank of England paper.*" This answer was admitted, as it suited the system of the Committee; to superstruct the Country Banks on the Bank of England; as if there were some interest, derived, by the one, from the others, to insinuate, rather than say, that the Bank of England is answerable, in payment, for the Country-bank paper: Yet, is Mr. Richardson's answer, thus admitted, without any explanation, *unsound.* The proper answer had been, to say; because, during the last *thirty* years, and upwards, a great spirit has gone forth, for improving the face of the country; so as to create much more business: The towns are improved, the roads are made, or mended, canals, and harbours, have been constructed; commons, wastes, and fens, have been divided, manuranced, and drained; and all those great country improvements have been performed, by private persons, at an an expence, which defies calculation*. But, from what person, and place, was the money derived? The Corporations, which busied themselves, in improving their towns, borrowed the money wanted, from capitalists, who had money to lend: The Trustees of the Roads, in the same manner, and under the same authority, borrowed their money of persons, who had money to lend. The constructing of the canals, and harbours, brought into action many personages of great importance, in every view, the rich nobility, and country gentlemen, whose lands were to be benefited, by such improvements, who laid out their money, and induced others to contribute†. The commons, wastes, and fens, were

* In the 10 Sessions, which ended with that of 1793, there were 626 Acts passed, for local purposes. From the Parliamentary record, it appears, that, there were enacted Statutes, for making local improvements, in Great Britain, in the eight years,

| | | | |
|---|---|---|---|
| Ending with | 1792 | - - - - | 750 |
| In D° | 1802 | - - - - | 1,124 |
| In D° | 1809 | - - - - | 1,444 |
| In 24 years, | | - - - - the N° | 3,318 |

All those improvements of our country were made, with the previous consent, and authority of Parliament; and leave was given by Parliament, to borrow money, for making those local improvements: So that, there is a *vast property* invested, in those establishments, under the authority of Parliament.

† At the dawn of commerce, in this island, the nobility, and gentry, were the chief capitalists, the monied men, whom, we see,

were improved, by the money of similar parties. (6.) We thus see prodigious capitals employed, in every shire, in the most beneficial manner; the country was thus improved; and high profits were obtained, upon the capitals, so employed: We now perceive that, as *money makes money*, according to the adage, so capitals, thus usefully employed, reproduced other capitals: Hence, after all those improvements, in the several shires, had made some progress, and personal property had been collected into great masses, a strong foundation was, thereby, laid, for the Country Banks, without any *superstructure* on the Bank of England: Hence, also, by a necessary consequence, the augmentation of Country-bank paper was much less owing to the augmentation of Bank notes, as the Committee supposes, than to the vast extension of country business, and internal commerce. The trade of the country, thus augmented, and increasing, necessarily promoted the dealings, and traffick of the metropolis: And, hence too, the augmentation of Bank notes, during the thirteen years of the Bank restriction, may be also owing, greatly, to those vast improvements of a local nature, and the internal business consequent thereon, full as much, perhaps, as to foreign trade: From the foregoing detail, we may

see, in lists of all the great trading Companies, and colonial Companies, during the reigns of Elizabeth, and James.—My Estimate on this point.

at

at length conclude, that Mr. Richardson, and the Committee, substituted the effect for the cause, when they took it for granted, that the augmentation of country discounts, was owing to the augmentation of Bank notes, rather than to the augmentation of country capitals, the necessary result of *reproduction*, from those vast enterprizes, in every shire, for local meliorations. It was these capitals, and that demand for money, which created the Country paper, and those discounts, by Country Bankers, during the last thirteen years of Bank restriction, and national prosperity, tenfold more, than during ages of sloth, and inactivity. (7.) The Committee, it should seem, can only contemplate the Bank restriction, as an evil: But, all those observations, with regard to the vast detail of country affairs, apply equally to the augmented business of our immense metropolis. Though the Bank has improved its modes, and increased its facilities; though the private Bankers have thereby acquired additional accommodations; yet, such is the vast augmentation of business; from change of habit, in rich individuals; from the increase of manufactures; from the vast augmentation of trade, domestic, and foreign; that there is still an increasing demand, for Bank notes, in the form of discounts, and other accommodations of business, to say nothing of the great public revenue, and the constant operations, in the money market, of the

the Sinking-fund Commissioners *. (8.) It had been nearer the fact, if the Committee had said, with its informants, that in a thousand instances, and to a large amount, the notes of the Country Banks had superseded the notes of the Bank of England; that thereby *securities for money* were substituted, for *cash*; and that a *bad* currency had been introduced, for a *good* one †: Yet, this gross abuse was not introduced, with the *consent* of the *Bank*; but, in *opposition* to the *resistance* of the Bank. Nothing can be more incongruous, in argument, than confounding Banks of different kinds together; the

* All those points were examined into, by the Lords Committee, in 1797: It was asked of Mr Irving, the then Inspector General, "Must not such an increase in the quantity of our "credits require a proportionate increase of capital; and must "not the employment of such increase of capital require an "increase, in the means of circulation? The increase of trade, "the Inspector General answered, necessarily requires an in-"crease of capital, and also an increase of money; because, I "conceive money is the *representation* of property; and in "proportion, as that property is increased, the necessity of in-"creasing such representation follows of course: By money, I "mean, either the precious metals, or paper, which has a si-"milar value affixed to it, by general consent." Report. 48. This answer, to a very important question, is solid and well worded.

† I have already proved this, by showing, that Bank notes are not in fact, increased, since the restriction, considering the defalcation of the gold coins, the increase of circulation, the augmentation of trade, domestic and foreign, the extension of of vast enterprizes, in every district, which created the Country Banks, that supplied the *medium*, which the Bank declined.

Bank

Bank of England, with the Banks of the Country; what is *stable*, with what is *unstable:* a Bank protected, by Statute, from paying specie, with Banks, that are not protected; except, absurdly mixing, by word, and writing, *securities for money*, with *cash:* According to the law of the land, as we have seen, *Bank notes* are not securities for *money*, but *cash*; the notes of the Country Banks, according to law, are *not cash*, but *securities* for *money*; and, as the people have sometimes felt, very *bad securities* for *money:* Yes; say the Committee, "the notes "of the Country Bankers are convertible, at the "option of the holders, into Bank of England "paper." But, how? The answer must be, by a *law-suit*. As the law, at present, stands, every holder of the paper of the Country Banks, or of the Banks of Scotland, has a right to demand payment of *such paper, in specie*, neither of those Banks being warranted, by Statute, like the Bank of England, from paying in specie; the Country Banker may offer, in consequence of such demand, *Bank notes:* The holder has a right to refuse them: And, being thus, *at issue*, a law-suit must ensue; the consequence of which must be, that the Court, and jury, must determine, who is right, in his pretension; and of course, *whether Country paper be convertible into Bank notes:* But, do this law-suit, and that altercation, constitute BANKING! Again: It is in evidence before the Committee, that there are at least, five million

million of Country paper, in circulation, *more* than Bank notes: How, then, are those five millions of Country notes *to be converted* into Bank notes, that do not exist? Now; is it not apparent, if there be a deficiency of Bank notes, in circulation, to the amount of five millions, admitting the convertibility of the Country paper, that the Country Bankers, if the nature of their securities do not entitle them to Bank discounts, that they must collect the floating *Bank notes*, in the country, at a *premium*, or *agio*; so that, at this moment, Bank notes, instead of being depreciated, are enhanced. We, at length, perceive, from those facts, and circumstances, that the position of the Committee cannot be maintained, either in its law, its fact, or its policy.

(14.) It has been already shown, that there is no relaxed management of the Bank, which is conducted now, as it has always been, with great additional experience, and some real improvements: It has been shown, that there has been *no excess*, in the *issue of notes*; considering the defalcation of the whole gold coins from trade, in 1797, the increase of commercial business, since that epoch, the augmentation of the public income, and general expenditure, the operations of the Sinking-fund Commissioners; and as a necessary consequence of all those energizing circumstances, the vast increase of the circulation, both in its amount, and rapidity, even though means have been found, to make cash payments,

ments, among Bankers, less frequent, and less cumbersome: (2.) The Bank restriction is not the effect of the *Bank desire*, as the Committee seem to admit; but, of the *consideration of Parliament* *. (3.) Whoever,

* In November 1797, that point came under the consideration of the House of Commons, when a Secret Committee was appointed, " to enquire, whether it be expedient further to " continue the *restriction* of two Acts, in the preceding Session, " respecting payments in cash by the Bank;" and that Committee soon after reported, among other matters, as follows: " Your Committee further find, that the course of exchange " with Hamburgh is, at present, *unusually favourable* to this " country, and that, from the situation of our trade, there is " good reason to imagine it will *so continue*, unless political " circumstances should occur to affect it.—Your Committee " next proceeded to examine the Governor, and Deputy Go- " vernor of the Bank, as to their opinion of the inconvenience, " which may have arisen, from the restriction imposed on the " Bank, from making payment in cash, and of the expediency " of continuing such restriction; and your Committee find, " that they are not aware of any such inconvenience, and that " they are supported, in that idea, by knowing that, the Bankers " and traders of London, who had a right, by the Act of Par- " liament, to demand three-fourths of any deposit, *in cash*, " which they had made, in the Bank, of £. 500. or upwards, " have only claimed about *one-sixteenth*: And, your Commit- " tee find, that the Court of Directors of the Bank, did on the " 26th of October 1797, come to the following Resolution:— " ' RESOLVED, That it is the Opinion of this Court, That the " Governor and Company of the Bank of England are enabled " to issue specie, in any manner, that may be deemed neces- " sary, for the accommodation of the public; and the Court " have no hesitation to declare, that the affairs of the Bank " are in such a state, that it can with safety resume its ac- " customed functions, if the political circumstances of the " country do not render it inexpedient: But, the Directors " deeming

(3.) Whoever, then, pushes against *the Bank restriction,* strikes at the wisdom of Parliament; which, after well weighing all circumstances, has enacted, that it shall continue during the present war, "the avowed purpose of the enemy being to "wound this country, by means of its *public credit,* "and

"deeming it foreign, to their province, to judge of those points, "wish to submit to the wisdom of Parliament, whether, as "it has been once judged proper to lay a restriction on the "payments of the Bank, in specie, it may, or may not, be "prudent to continue the same.'"—"Your Committee having "further examined the Governor, and Deputy Governor, as "to what may be meant, by the political circumstances men-"tioned, in that Resolution, find, that they understand by them "the state of hostility, in which the nation is still involved; "and particularly such apprehensions as may be entertained "of invasion, either in Ireland, or this country, together with "the possibility there may be of advances being to be made, "from this country to Ireland; and that from those circum-"stances so explained, and from the nature of the war, and "*the avowed purpose* of *the enemy,* to *attack* this *country,* by "*means* of its *public credit,* and to distress it, in its *financial* "*operations,* they [the Committee] are led to think, that it "will be expedient to continue the restriction now subsisting, "with the reserve, for partial issues of specie, at the discretion "of the Bank, of the nature of those contained, in the present "Acts; and that it may be so continued, without injury to *the* "*credit of* the *Bank,* and *with advantage* to *the nation*:—Your "Committee, therefore, having taken into consideration the "general situation of the country, are of opinion, that notwith-"standing the affairs of the Bank, both with respect to the "general balance of its accounts, and its capacity of making "payments in specie, are in such a state, that it might with "safety resume its accustomed functions, under a different state "of public affairs; yet, that it will be expedient to continue, "the

"and to *distress* it, in its *financial operations*." (4.) And, as no commercial, or financial inconveniences had been felt, from that restriction, in November 1797, or in December 1803; so none has been made out, in evidence, on the late enquiry; the *Country-bank system* having existed *before*, and the *abuses* of that *system* having arisen, from very different causes, than the Bank restriction, as we have already seen, felt, and lamented. Every examination of fact, and every result of experience, establish a very different position: May it not, then, be asked, how far the domestic manufacture of the precious metals has been lessened, or augmented, before, or since, the restriction? The answer must be, that it has greatly increased; for, in the 10 years, ending with 1797, when there was *no* Bank restriction, there were made into *gold* plate, in this nation - - - - - - lbs. 10,171

In the 10 years, ending with 1809, when there *was* a Bank restriction, there were made - - - - - 16,942.

In

" the restriction, now subsisting on such payments, for such " time, and under such limitations, as to the wisdom of Par- " liament may seem fit." [This Report was ordered to be printed, on the 17th of November 1797.] In pursuance of all those considerations, the restriction was continued, from time to time, till the 15th of December 1803, when by the Act, 44 G. iii. ch. 1. the Bank restriction was continued, during the present war, and for six months, after the return of peace.

In the 1st period, there was made of *silver* plate - - - - - 919,283

In the 2d period, there were made of the same - - - - - 1,130,451.

Such, then, was the increase of the domestic manufacture of *plate*, in the *two* periods: But, has not every other manufacture equally increased, in the *last* period, *more* than in the *first?* Yes. Has not our foreign trade equally increased, in the last period? Yes*. Are not those proofs then, so many results of experience, that our commercial affairs have prospered, under that restriction? The Committee thinks otherwise, contrary to this experience, and to those proofs.

(15.) The Committee declares, that the rules, by which the Bank makes its discounts, are "sound, "and well established principles:" But, the Committee, also, says, "that the opinions confidently "expressed by the Bank Directors, and the mer-"chants, as far as such opinions go, to prove that "these rules cannot lead to any excess of Bank "notes in circulation, appears to the Committee "to be a doctrine wholly erroneous, in principle, and "pregnant with dangerous consequences, in prac-"tice †." The Committee goes on to say, that so long as "the Bank paper was convertible into

* See the Chron. Table, Appx. N° 1. for the most ample proofs of the nation's prosperity, under the Bank restriction.

† Report, 21.

"specie,

"specie, at the will of the holder, the rules, by "which the Bank were guided, in making its dis- "counts, and issuing notes, *were sufficient*; but, "that *since* the suspension of payments, in specie, "these are insufficient." The Committee immediately adds that, "to watch the operations of so "new a law, and to provide against the injury, "which might result from it to the public interest, "was the province, not so much of *the Bank*, as of "the *Legislature*; in the opinion of the Committee, "there is room to regret, that this house has not "taken earlier notice of all the consequences of "that law *." After reading those strong opinions of the Committee, both with regard to the *Legislature*, and the *Bank*, we may ask whether they be founded in knowledge; (1.) Did the Legislature, then, apply no remedy to the grievance of that day? The grand grievance, which was then complained of, both by the Bank Directors, and private Bankers, was the vast, and constant *advances* to the Treasury, which prevented the abundance of discounts to the merchants, and Bankers, for commercial purposes: Now, the Restraining Act of 1797 †, did, by an express clause, provide, that during the continuance of the restriction, the Bank should not, in any one year, advance more than £. 600,000, for the public service, on the credit of *Exchequer bills*: Then, what

* Ib. 22—3.

† 37 G. iii. ch. 45—§ iv.

was

was the amount of the grievance, which was thus remedied by the Legislature? The answer must be, an annual advance upon the credit of Exchequer bills, according to a six years average, ending with 1796, of £. 5,531,983 *: We may now perceive, that the above remedy did reserve to the Bankers, and merchants, for their usual accommodation, an annual sum, amounting nearly to *five million* of pounds: And, did not the Commons House take early notice of the consequences of that law? Yes; there was a Secret Committee of that house, which sat, in November 1796 [the above Statute was passed in May preceding] to enquire into the expediency of further continuing that restriction, as we have seen above, whose Report was printed, on the 17th of the same month of November, in favour of the restriction, though the Directors offered to open the Bank for payments, in specie; and this Secret Committee laid before the House a very memorable fact, that those bodies of men, who had a right, under that Statute, to demand specie, did not call for *one-sixteenth* of what they were entitled to: The restriction, then, was continued, as it appeared to be of great importance, as it might be done, "*without* any *injury* to the *credit* of the *Bank*, and "*with advantage* to the *nation*:" What, then, does the outcry of the Bullion Committee amount to, but, that it thinks differently, with regard to the

† Lords' Report, Appx. 13.

credit

credit of the Bank, and the advantage of the nation, from the Secret Committee of November 1797; and blames the Legislature of May 1797, without just cause: Comparisons however, of men, and characters, are odious, says the adage. (2.) As to the security of the public; we have already seen, that there is every just motive, to restrain an excessive issue of Bank notes: It is the *interest* of the Bank, not to issue more, than the circulation of the country, easily, receives; it is the interest of merchants, and Bankers, not to ask, for more discounts, than they can make an advantageous use of; and the richest merchant, or Banker, is limited to a certain sum, beyond which, the Bank will not discount, for him: Neither does the Bank discount for any one, but *paper* of a particular kind, which comes round the circle, soon, and certainly, to payment: The Committee was, also, assured by the Governor, and Deputy Governor, that the Bank *never forces* a note into circulation; and there will not a note more remain, in circulation, than is immediately wanted; and if the Bank were to issue notes, beyond the real wants of circulation, the surplus would immediately return to the Bank: Now, these facts point to the satisfactory security of the public, against excessive issues, the daily vibrations of *demand*, and *supply*; because, a great demand, and a small supply, would raise the value of the notes, in the circle; but, a great supply, and a small demand, would deteriorate them: It is thus, that the *demand*, and *supply*,

*supply*, regulate every market, even for the precious metals, as much as for any merchandizes, or other goods: And, it was specially stated to the Committee, on this head, by the Governors of the Bank, "We have 'daily evidence, in our discounting, of the abundance, or scarcity, of Bank notes, by the application for discounts, for the reasons already "assigned; which is particularly proved, by our "experience on the Tuesdays, and Wednesdays, in "every week, in consequence of our discounting "London paper, on the *Thursdays only*; producing, by that operation, invariably, a certain "degree of scarcity, on the two preceding days, and "a plenty, on the following day *." The Committee, "however, is of opinion, "that mercantile discounts to whatever amount cannot be regarded "as any other, than a great public benefit; and that "it is only the excess of paper currency, thereby "issued, and kept out in circulation, which is to be

Com. Minutes, 97; 119;—121; 142-3:—It was the opinion of the very intelligent Mr. Greffulhe, who spoke, throughout, with the neutrality of a stranger, "that there does exist, "under the Restriction, the same security against excessive "issues, that there did before, if the Bank, strictly, adhere to the "system of discounting, which has been long in use." Ib. 72. Sir F. Baring being asked his opinion, if any adequate provision could be made against excessive issues, in a commercial country, where the paper is not convertible into specie, said, "In "this country, if I may judge, from experience, I should doubt "it; but, if the Bank conduct itself, on the same principles, "as formerly, I should think, that it may be safely left to the "discretion

"be considered, as the evil *." But, how to enjoy the *good*, without the accompanying *evil*, is one of the hardest tasks of metaphysicks to prescribe. The best things, are generally accompanied with the worst inconveniences. Liberty cannot be enjoyed, without sometimes feeling the inconvenience of licentiousness: Religion sometimes degenerates into superstition: Yet, such disquisitions are more fit for the Schools, than the Senate House.

The Committee now lament, that the Bank Directors, under the restriction, are invested with the full trust, and the important charge, of supplying the whole country, with that quantity of circulating medium, which is exactly proportioned to the occasions, and wants of the public; but, it thinks this a trust, which is beyond the ability of the Directors to discharge, with adequate proportion to the end †. But, is this *true* in point of *fact?* It is in evidence, that there is, in circulation, more paper of the Country Banks, than there is Bank cash, by *five millions* sterling: But, have the Bank Directors any thing to do with the direction, in the issue of five and twenty million of Country-bank securities for money? Thus, loosely, does the Committee report, when it tried to be metaphysically precise. But, the Committee, on this head,

"discretion of the Bank." Ib. 131. The Committee seems to leave out of the queſtion the general superintendance of Parliament over all such establishments.

* Ib. 63. 8° edit.

† Report, 24.

entirely

entirely overlooked the Country Banks; and made the Bank Directors answerable for all; though Mr. Stukey, who said, he is a partner, in three Country Banks, expressly stated to the Committee, that the Country Banks do not regulate their issues, by the amount of the Bank notes, which are in the circle*. But, who did not know this fact, before Mr. Stukey informed the Committee of it; who, at last, did not believe him? It was this Mr. Stukey, thus a respectable partner, in *three Country Banks*, who told the Committee, moreover, upon being asked his opinion, that the prices of all things are raised, by the abundant circulation, but chiefly, by Bank notes: But, with submission to Mr. Stukey, is it not fair to argue that, as Bank notes are *cash*, and Country paper, but *securities* for money, every seller will give his goods cheaper for cash, than for *securities* for money. (6.) "The Committee, however, declares "that, in their judgment, the Directors of the Bank "of England have exercised the new, and extraordi-"nary trust reposed in them, since 1797, with an in-"tegrity, and regard to the public interest, accord-"ing to their conceptions of it, and indeed a degree "of forbearance, in turning it less to the profit of "the Bank, than it would easily have admitted "of, that merit the continuance of that confidence, "which the public has so long, and so justly felt, in

* Minutes, 140.

"the

" the integrity, with which its affairs are directed, " as well as, in the unshaken stability, and ample " funds of that great establishment*." The proper question, is, however, with submission, not whether it be possible, according to fancied theory, to adjust the quantity of circulating medium, *exactly*; but, whether the practical rules, which are always acted on, by the Directors, in making their discounts, and issues, be right, and the best, that can, all circumstances considered, be followed: The Bankers, and merchants, who have been examined now, and formerly, in 1797, plainly state, that, in their judgements, they are so; and the Bank Directors declare, that practical experience has taught them, that they are the fittest, and most approved; Yet, does the Committee controvert the sufficiency of these practical rules†; and insist, that a more sure criterion must be resorted to; and such a criterion, the Committee professes to have already shown, which is to be found, in the state of the exchanges, and in the price of bullion‡: Whereupon, " the Committee reports it to the House, as their clear " opinion, that so long as the suspension of cash " payments is permitted to subsist, the price of " gold bullion, and the general exchanges with " foreign countries, taken for any considerable " period of time, form the best general criterion, " from which any inference can be drawn, as to the

* Report, 24. † Ib. 22—3. ‡ Id; Ib. 27.

" sufficiency,

"sufficiency, or excess, of paper money, in circula-
"tion; and that the Bank of England cannot safely
"regulate the amount of its issues, without having
"reference to the criterion, presented, by these two
"circumstances*." The whole reasoning of the Committee, whereon is founded that *clear opinion*, may be compressed into this brief formulary: The Committee assumes, that the increase of Bank notes has produced the high price of gold bullion, with the depression of the exchanges; and *vice versa* the Committee infers, from a sort of cross deduction, that the high price of gold bullion, with the low exchanges, show the excess of Bank notes: But, as it has been proved, both, by *testimony*†, and the *fact*, that the amount of Bank notes, in circulation, has no effect on the rate of the foreign exchanges, or the price of gold bullion, it is most clear, in argument, that the circumstances, which the Committee have reported to the House, "as the best general crite-
"rion," of the sufficiency, or excess of paper currency, in circulation, is a most mistaken criterion.

(7.) The Committee is more fortunate, in its opinion of the *Bank's advances* to Government; for it reports, "that they have had an account laid before
"them of *advances* made by the *Bank* to *Govern-*
"*ment*, on land, and malt, Exchequer bills, and

* Report, 21.

† Minutes, 69, 71, 90—5, 96—7, 112, 143—4, &c. Appx. Rep. N° 47—9; my Appx. N° 2.

"other

"other *securities*, in every year, since the suspen-
"sion of cash paymenss; from which, as compared
"with the accounts, laid before the Committees of
"1797, and which were then carried back for 20
"years; it will appear, that the yearly advances of
"the Bank to Government have, upon an average,
"since the suspension, been considerably lower in
"amount, than the average amount of advances,
"prior to that event; and the amount of those ad-
"vances, in the two last years, though greater in
"amount, than those of some years, immediately
"preceding, is less, than it was, for any of the six
"years, preceding the restriction*:" These representations, then, exhibit to the House very important facts; as they prove that, the advances, by the Bank, to Government, have been much smaller, *since the* restriction; while the expenditure of Government, and the general circulation, and commerce of the country, have greatly increased: Now; the Bankers, and merchants, who were examined, both, in 1797, and in 1810, concur, in stating it, as a point indisputable, that whatever diminution is made, in the advances of the Bank to Government, must be added, as a good, to general circulation, and trade, domestic, and foreign, by enlarging the discounts to merchants: So, on the other hand, any *great restriction* of the circulating medium would produce great, and general public distress, by impeding cir-

* Report 25—6; Appx. No. 45.

culation,

culation, the very worst evil, that can afflict a commercial, and manufacturing people *.

(15). The Acts of Parliament, restricting the payments, in specie, of the Bank, do *not* protect the Banks, in Scotland, from paying, in specie, when demanded †; nor, do the same Acts protect the country banks of England, from paying, in specie, if required; then, how are they protected, from demands, for specie? they are protected, in no other manner, than all other persons are protected:

* See the Min. Lords Com. and of the Common's Com. 1797; and of the Bullion Com. 1810.

† The evidence of the Banker, Mr. Mansfield, to the Committee on Irish exchanges, Report, 51. "It will be convenient "also, says the Bullion Report, in its concluding paragraph, "for the chartered Banks of Ireland, and Scotland, and all the "Country Banks, that they should not be compelled to pay, in "specie, until some time after the resumption, of payments by "the Bank of England; but, that they should continue, for a "short period, upon their present footing, of being liable to "pay their own notes, on demand, in Bank of England *paper*." Report, 8° edit. 78. We thus see, that the Committee was of opinion, the *Banks of Scotland*, and the *Country Banks*, are *now restricted* from paying, in specie, like the Bank of England, and the Bank of Ireland. But, the Committee is mistaken, both in the law, and the fact: For, the Banks of Scotland, and the Country Banks, are not restricted, by any Statute, from paying in specie; and any one may demand specie of either; and the recommendation of the Committee goes to protect both, after the restriction shall be removed, from the Bank of England. The Committee is, moreover, mistaken, in its law, when it calls *Bank notes*, *paper*, instead of *cash*. The whole paragraph is an egregious error, both in law, and policy.

(2.) The

(2.) The Country Banks, if specie were demanded of them, may, and so may every one else, offer the amount of the demand, in *Bank notes*, which, according to law, are *cash;* and it would be an absurd construction of the *custom of trade*, and of the *common law*, to say, under our circumstances, that Bank notes, which, according to both, are cash, *are not* an acquittal, for any demand, except for something agreed on, by specific promise. (3.) When Mr. Gilchrist was asked, by the Bullion Committee, whether the Bank notes, in Scotland, had increased, *since* the *Bank restriction*, he answered, like an intelligent man, "I think the paper circulation of "Scotland has increased, since that period; in "consequence of the increased trade of the country, and of the extensive agricultural improvements of Scotland*." A similar answer might be given, as to the augmented circulation of the Country-bank *paper*, though I have shown the unsoundness of the answer of Mr. Richardson, when he attributed the augmented discounts to the increase of Country-bank paper, and Bank notes: Augmented *dealings* will require an augmented circulation; and augmented dealings, with an augmented circulation, would naturally give rise to additional discounts: Yet, none of those effects are to be attributed, in fair discussion, to the Bank restriction; but, to country improvements, to extended

* Report, 8° edit. 160.

manufactures,

manufactures, and to an enlarged trade, which necessarily require more money, either good, or bad; and it has been shown above, that, as far as *Bank cash* has been excluded, by the substitution of *securities for money*, there exists, in our Country circulating medium, a *gross abuse*; but, none in the *Bank cash*: The Committee, then, fails egregiously in *not* pointing the attention of the House to *the Country Banks*, rather than to the Bank of England, in which there is no perceivable abuse, at least, in the eyes of *practical* men, whatever there may be, in the *ken* of *theoretick* men, "strech'd out to the "amplest reach of prospect."

(16.) What, then, are the chief abuses of the Country Banks, there being none, in the Bank of England, or in the Banks of Scotland? (1.) The number of 700 Country Banks, and upwards, are much too many; as in such a number of traders, ten, or a dozen, must become bankrupts, in every year; and when an impeded circulation happens, a hundred may fail, as a hundred Country Bankers became bankrupts, in 1793; so that proportional discredit is thus cast upon the whole system of Banking: And, this is a terrible abuse, to which some remedy ought to be applied. (2.) If a Country Bank lends money upon mortgage, or other securities, which cannot be, readily, converted into *cash*; this transforms such an establishment into a *Land* Bank: Now, we have had *Land Banks* fail, in England; and the Air Bank,

in

in Scotland, failed*; because it was a *Land Bank:* And land is an improper capital, for Banks, issuing notes payable to bearer; which require *cash*, to satisfy daily demands, and not *securities for money.* (3.) In the same manner, notes payable to bearer, optionally, some days after presentation, for payment, or at some other Bank, specified in the notes, may be good *securities* for money; but, they are *not money;* much less are they *cash*, like the *Bank notes*: (4.) Let the practice of the Country Banks be put, by Statute, on the footing of the Banks, in Scotland, and the specified abuses will evanish, as such abuses disappeared, in Scotland, when such a Statute prohibited all elusory clauses, and laxity of practice†: It is quite wonderful, how the Committee, as we have seen, constantly runs at *the Bank of England,* in which there is no relaxation of management, or excess of any kind, as the Committee acknowledges, while it scarcely casts a sidelong glance at the Country Banks, in which prevail every abuse; the abuse of numbers, the abuse of laxity;

* In 1694, a *Land* Bank failed, in England. Anderson's Deduction, ii. 291. The value of the lands, which were the grounds of the Air Bank, were of fifty times more, than its debts: But, it failed; because it did not so much want *security*, as *cash*: It finally paid every claim; since it had value enough, but wanted time, to convert *securities* into *cash.*

† 5 Geo. iii. ch. 49. See Mr. Mansfield's evidence, in the Report of the Committee, on Irish Exchanges.

the

the obscurity of their establishments, and the excess of their issues.

(17.) But, why close such strictures on the Bank of England, without any animadversions, on the Country Banks, which lie open to censure, by recommending the removal of the Bank restriction, which introduced so much positive good; and which the Secret Committee of the Commons House said had existed, *without any injury to the credit of the Bank*, and *with so much advantage to the nation?* Was not the Bank restriction recommended, by several Committees of both Houses of Parliament, consisting of men of full as much knowledge, and experience, as any other Committee ever possessed? Has not the wisdom of Parliament, after repeated trials of its salutariness, determined, by a solemn Act*, that the Bank restriction shall not be repealed, during a war, which is professedly carried on against our commerce, our credit, both public, and private, and our financial operations. Is it not a fact, which stands recorded, in the proceedings of Parliament, that the bodies of men, who, under the Restriction Act, had a right, to ask for specified sums of specie, never applied, for one *sixteenth part* of what Parliament had allowed them? What a *fact* is here, in support of *experience*, which is

* 44 G. iii. ch. 1.

oppugned

oppugned by *metaphysics!* Has the nation ever advanced more prosperously, in all that constitute industry, agriculture, commerce, opulence, and greatness, during the period of the Bank restriction, thirteen years of malignant hostilities! Have we ever executed, in any other period, so many local improvements? Were there ever more skill, and capital employed, in husbandry? Had we ever so much manufacture, before, even of *gold* and *silver plate*, though not of coins? Did we ever export, within the year, the surplus products of our land, and labour, to the real value of SIXTY-SIX MILLIONS? Did our public income, in any age, yield so much into the Exchequer? Did we ever obtain loans for the state, on lower terms? Did we ever, in such a length of years, liquidate so much of the public debts? Did the national securities, or stocks, ever rise so high, during former wars, under different auspices, when hostilities were not waged against our trade, for destroying our private credit abroad, and lessening the public credit at home? The Parliamentary accounts verify the foregoing representations of truth, which forbid the removal of the Bank restriction; so as to allow the export of gold, that would only have the effect, of making gold bullion dear, at home, and cheap abroad. After seeing *theory* so often substituted, for *experience*, well may we exclaim with Pope;—

"See Metaphysicks call, for aid, on Sense."

---

The

## The Conclusion.

The Committee, at length, after, deliberately, considering this subject, thought proper, to report to the Commons House, as its opinion: (1.) That the system of the circulating medium of this country ought to be brought back, with as much speed, as is compatible, with a wise and necessary caution, to the original principle of *cash payments*, at the option of the holder of *Bank paper*. (2.) According to the best judgment, which the Committee has been able to form, no sufficient remedy, for the present, or security for the future, can be pointed out, except the *repeal* of *the law*, which *suspends* the *cash payments* of the Bank of England: (3.) Under every view, the Committee would suggest, that the restriction of cash payments cannot, safely, be removed, at an earlier period, than two years, from the present time; but, the Committee was of opinion, that early provision ought to be made, by Parliament, for terminating, by the end of that period, the operation of the several Statutes, which have imposed, and continued the restriction *.

But, to this recommendation, and to those reasons, may be objected the following considerations: 1. It is perfectly obvious, that the whole Report of the Bullion Committee is opposed by the *two* Reports of the *Secret Committees*, of the Lords, and

* Report, 8° ed. 74—6.

Commons,

Commons, 1797, after enquiries of equal anxiety, and at length submitted to both Houses, with deliberate consideration, quite equal to that of the Bullion Committee: This Report is also made, without any notice of the Report of the Commons Secret Committee, in November 1797, which reported these two strong grounds, for continuing the Bank restriction, that it might be done, without *injury to the credit* of *the Bank*, and *with advantage* to the *nation;* considering, moreover, the *existing hostility*, and *nature* of *the war*, as well as the avowed purpose of the enemy, "to attack this "country, by means of its public credit, and to "distress it, in its financial operations:" Now; all those powerful motives, which have not been answered, in any manner, induced the concentrated wisdom of the whole Parliament, in December 1803, to continue the Bank restriction, throughout the present war, and six months, after its conclusion: Here, then, is a Parliamentary pledge to the whole world, that the restriction, which had been found to be salutary, should be so long enforced: And, the commercial people of the united nation of Great Britain, and Ireland, have, in carrying on their mercantile affairs, placed their firm trust, in that solemn pledge. 2. The consideration of the Bullion Committee was directed to *three* heads; the *high price* of *gold bullion*; the foreign *ex-*

*changes*,

*changes;* the *state* of the *circulating medium:* And, of all these, in their order.

1. With regard to the *price* of *bullion,* the Committee represent that, "during the *twenty-* "*four* years, *preceding* the *restriction,* the price "of Gold Bullion continued remarkably *steady,* at "something *below* the Mint price, with a very few "exceptions, to a small amount *." But, these were "ordinary times," say the Committee; and, without hostility to trade, enmity to exchangers, and the most insidious warfare on the private credit, and public revenue of the British nation, the Committee might have added. We are thus led on to enquire, whether the Committee be founded, or unfounded, in the *assumption* of the *low prices* of gold bullion, before the memorable epoch of the Bank restriction: We must always recollect, that the Mint price of gold is £. 3. 17*s.* 10½*d.* per oz.; while the Bank price is £. 3. 17*s.* 6*d*, which, appearing on the face of the Bank statement of prices, to be very inferior, probably misled the Committee *.

Now;

* Report, 4.

† Let us now examine the prices of gold, in the years preceding 1797: Mr. Giles, the Governor of the Bank, stated to the Commons' Secret Committee, in 1797, "that in 1772, "the Bank bought some gold for £. 4. 1. and £. 4. 2. per oz.; and, that more recently the Bank imported some gold coin, from Lisbon, which cost them £. 4. 6. per oz. and which they sold again, for the most part, for export to the West Indies, at £. 4. 4. [Minutes, 148.] Mr. Ab. Newland stated

Now; as all those extraordinary prices were previous to the Bank restriction, when, according to the Committee's doctrine, there could not be an excess of Bank notes, it follows, from the fact, that those high prices could not have arisen, from the excess, and *supposed depreciation*; but, in truth, from the natural course of trade, and the usual vibrations of demand, and supply, in the London market, as settled by the popular voice: And, we may thus perceive, from all those facts, and circumstances, as to the *high prices* of gold, previous to the Bank restriction, that the Committee's doctrine is completely invalidated. Again: The Bank notes increased, from £. 9,985,220, in 1796, to £, 10,403,000, in 1797, and to £. 12,695,970, in 1798; augmentations these, which should have produced, according to the Committee's doctrine a rise, in the price of *gold* bullion; and yet, we know from the fact, that the price of British standard gold was in 1798, and 1799, £. 3. 19*s*. 6*d*.

stated to the Lords' Committee, in 1797, that in various prior years, the Bank had given for gold £. 4. 1, £. 4. 2, £. 4. 6, and once, about 1795, £. 4. 8. per oz.; but, that the Bank seldom bought at these prices; yet, that, within the last two years, gold had been at a higher price than £. 4. 4. per oz. [Minutes, 67—8.] On the 8th of October 1795, the Governor of the Bank stated, in a communication to the Chancellor of the Exchequer, that the price of gold then was £. 4. 4. per oz. Mr. Hoare, the Banker, stated to the Commons Committee, in March 1797, that the price of gold was so high, that a guinea was worth, as bullion, from 22 to 24 shillings, abroad. [Minutes, 86.]

per oz. and of foreign gold £. 4; while, in 1795, and 1796, before the restriction took place, gold was upwards of £. 4. 4. per oz. and the average amount of the Bank notes was £. 9,985,220, to £. 10,910,390 *. From those facts, we now perceive, that while the amount of Bank notes was progressively *increasing*, the price of gold was progressively *decreasing*: And this striking contradiction, to the Committee's theory, continued throughout the six following years down to 1808: For, during the 5 years, from 1804 to 1808, the market price of gold continued, at £. 4. per oz. while Bank notes increased to the average amount of £. 16,673,710.

(9.) It was only, in the latter end of 1808, that the price of gold began to rise; owing to a deficiency of the supply, and a great increase, in the demand, from the Continent. It was proved to the Committee, by those who knew the fact, that of the gold sold, in the London market, less than a 20th part is sold for exportation †; and that more than 20 parts is sold, for exportation ‡. And, it was, also, proved to the Committee, that the prices of gold, in the London market, are regulated, by the prices abroad §.

* In 1800 gold sold for £. 4. 5. to £. 4. 6. per oz.: in 1801, for £. 4. 6, £. 4. 5, £. 4. 4. 6; £. 4. 4, £. 4. 3. 6, £. 4. 3, and £. 4. 2. 6. per oz.; and, in 1802, gold sold for £. 4. 3. 6, and £. 4. 2. 9. per oz.: Now; during these 3 years, the average amount of Bank notes, in the circle, was in 1800 £. 14,563,740; in 1801, £. 15,459,050; and in 1802, £. 16,320,950.

† Minutes of Evid. 39. ‡ Id. § Ib. 65.

The

The foregoing efficient facts clearly prove, that the *assumed theory* of the Committee, as to the increase, or decrease, of *Bank notes*, ruling the prices of gold, is altogether unfounded, and I was going to say, irrational. But, I have already exhibited this topick of *the prices* of *bullion*, in such a variety of lights, that, I trust, every fair enquirer, must see, that the late high prices may be attributed to any other causes, than what the Committee has adopted, as *a theory*. I will only beg leave to add the deliberate judgment of the late Joseph Harris, the celebrated Assay-master of the Mint, on the question, whether *bullion* can be regarded, as *a standard*, or *measure**: "As *bullion*, says this able writer, "occurs much more than *coin*, in the transactions "of merchants; some of them have been induced, "from thence to think, that the *price* of *bullion* is "what governs, and *measures*, the *value* of all *other* "*things*. But, from what hath been already delivered, it is very manifest, that the *price* of *bullion* "is *governed* as well as *measured*, by *coin*, or the "established *standard of money*; and not suffered "to *deviate much*, from that *standard*. With "merchants, indeed, any commodity they deal in, "may be said, indifferently, to be a standard, for all "the rest, as well as gold, or silver; for they consider all things; as they will purchase more, or "less, of each the other, in this place, or in that;

* Essay on Money, part ii, p. 64.

"and

"and coins, which with the rest of the world is "money, is with them thrown into the general "hotch-potch, and no otherwise distinguished, from "other commodities, but from the proportion, that "certain quantities of one, or the other, will fetch "of the rest; and they join with us rather in lan-"guage, than in idea, as to the use of coins: No "wonder then, if such gentlemen treat the *standard* "*of money* so slightly, and so *disdainfully*, as some "of them do." We may thus perceive, then, that this great master had exploded the *absurd theory* of *bullion* being a *standard*, or *measure*, more than fifty years, before the Bullion Committee adopted it, in opposition to facts, and in contempt of experience.

(2.) From the doctrines of bullion, to the question of the unfavourable exchanges, the transition is easy: I have, already, in the foregoing sheets laid before the inquisitive reader this perplexing question, in almost every possible light: And, it has been shown, distinctly, that the *true equilibrium* of the exchanges is the *export* of *goods*, *rather* than *bullion*, when goods can be sent to the *proper port*; as we abound, in merchandizes, both native, and foreign, which we can command; but, bullion, which we cannot command, does *not* by any means abound, when compared with the demand: And yet, have the Committee assumed, as a truth, what has not been proved, as a fact, that the *deprecia-*
tion

*tion* of *the Bank notes* has produced the *depression* of the *exchanges*, however contradicted, by proofs, and by argument; by theory, and practice: Although, however, the Committee has assumed this egregious errour, throughout the examination of the evidence, and in various parts of the Report, yet when they found that the facts were against them, and came to explain their notion more specially, they qualify it by admitting that, " on the whole, " they are *not of opinion, that a material depression* " *of the exchanges has been manifestly to be traced* " *in its amount and degree to an augmentation of* " *notes corresponding in point of time.* They con- " ceive that the more minute and *ordinary fluctua-* " *tions of exchange are generally referable to the* " *course of our commerce*; that political events, " operating upon the state of trade, may often have " contributed as well to the rise as to the fall of " the exchange; and in particular, that the first " remarkable depression of it, in the beginning of " 1809, is to be ascribed, as has been stated, in the " evidence already quoted, to commercial events, " arising out of the occupation of the North of " Germany by the troops of the French Emperor. " *The evil has been that the exchange, when fallen,* " *has not had the full means of recovery under the* " *subsisting system**." It would have been more fit, to have stated the real fact, that the great depression

* Report, p. 16.

of

of the exchange, in 1809, is to be ascribed, to commercial events, *arising out of the restrictions imposed by the French Emperor on our trade, and communication with the Continent*, in consequence of his occupation of the North of Germany; *and that it has not had the full means of recovery, owing to the continuance, and increased rigor of those restrictions*; whereby the export of goods, the proper equilibrium, could not be applied: Nor, will the exchanges ever be restored, to a much more favourable state, till that equilibrium be effectually applied. It has indeed been given in evidence to the Committee, that *the Bank restriction was no cause of the unfavourable course of the exchange*; *and that the removal of this restriction would not remedy the exchange*; also, that the increased amount of Bank notes, which the Committee ascribe to this restriction, has not caused the depression of the exchange; and that the diminution of Bank notes, which the Committee wish to produce, by the removal of the restriction, would not improve the exchange*: It has also been given in evidence to the Committee, that, as the export of our current money is prohibited, the only effectual means of recovering the exchange is by a free export of commodities †.

* See Minutes of Evidence, p. 112, 127, 71, 90, 95, 96—7, 143, 144, and passim.

† See Minutes of Evidence, passim.

(3.) With

(3.) With regard to the supposed excess of the *circulating medium*; I have already shown this topick, in such a variety of views to every intelligent reader of the foregoing Considerations, that I trust, it has appeared that there is really no excess in the *Bank cash*, whatever there may be in *Country Bank securities* for *money*: Yet, as this is a subject of great importance, I will beg leave to submit, that the assumption of the Committee, on this head, will appear to be wholly unfounded: Of all the merchants, and Bankers, who were examined by the Committee, on that most important topick, the late Sir Francis Baring was the only person, who joined in the Committee's opinion of there being any excess of *Bank cash*, in circulation at present *: His admission, however, of the general proposition, which was suggested to him in the question, that an increase of capital, commerce, agriculture, and public revenue, requires a proportionate increase of circulating medium, decides the question, against the opinion he gives of an excess of Bank notes: for the Bank notes have not nearly increased, in the same proportion, as the trade, and public revenue. The other merchants, and Bankers, who were examined on this point, state expressly, that there is no excess of Bank of England notes, and give very satisfactory reasons for this: They even go further, and state, that, while the Bank Directors adhere

* See the Minutes, 131.

strictly

strictly to the practical rule by which they give their discounts, and make their issues, there can be no excess of Bank notes *. The Bankers and merchants, who were examined by the Secret Committees of the Lords, and Commons, in 1797, also stated, that the increase of capital, commerce, manufactures, agriculture, public revenue, and expenditure of this country, necessarily required, a proportionate increase of circulating medium †. The same indisputable proposition was stated in evidence before the late Bullion Committee. It was, also, given in evidence before the Committee of 1797, that our commerce, in time of war, requires a greater capital, to carry it on, than in time of peace ‡. These propositions, then, being established, furnish a scale, for trying the progressive amount of Bank notes, whether they have been carried to an excess. This test the late Committee have not chosen to apply, but resorted to a theoretical inference, which they drew from the price of bullion, and the state of the exchanges, without adverting much to the

* See Minutes, p. 69, 71, 72, 102, 121, and passim.

† See Minutes of both, passim; and see, particularly, the evidence of Mr. Henry Thornton before the Lords Committee, Minutes, p. 71–2, 82; the evidence of Mr. Walter Boyd before the same, Ib. p. 114, and before the Commons Committee, Minutes, p. 52, 57; and the evidence of Mr. Thomas Irving, the Inspector General, before the Lords Committee, Minutes, p. 48.

‡ See Minutes of Lords Committee, p. 77, 114, &c.

evidence

evidence, which was given before them, on the point. It was said, in evidence, before the Committee, that the increase of Bank notes was fully accoutned for, and justified, by the groat increase of commerce, of the public revenue, and expenditure, and by the increased payments, in the metropolis*. Mr. Whitmore, the Governor of the Bank, stated to the Committee, that " the amount of Bank of England notes " during the last year, 1809, have borne exactly " the same proportion to the occasions of the pub" lic, as in former times.†" He also stated, to the Committee, that the payments made by the London Bankers, in Bank of England notes, in the course of one day, is considerably above five millions ‡. The Committee give a statement of the " average " amount of Bank of England notes in circulation, " in each year," from 1798 to 1809, inclusive. In this Statement, they improperly include *Bank Post Bills*, which cannot be considered, as current cash, being merely lent, as remittances, and return directly to the Bank for payment ‡. By this statement, the

* See Minutes passim, and particularly p. 71—2, 79, and 119.

† Minutes, p. 79. ‡ Ib. 121.

‡ During these twelve years the Bank Post Bills increased from about £.645,000, the average amount, in 1798, to £.895,815, the average amount, in 1809. This gives a pretty strong intimation of the increased circulation, during this period, and of course the want of an increase in the circulating medium. It must be remarked, that the increase, of Bank Post Bills is altogether uninfluenced by the Bank restriction; for whether the Bank pay, in specie, or in Bank notes, the amount of the Bank Post Bills will be the same, in correspondence.

Committee

Committee exhibits an increase of Bank notes, from £. 13,334,752, in 1798, to £. 19,991,890, in 1809. But, in this last amount, there is a very great error; for, the real average amount of Bank notes, including Bank Post Bills, in 1809, was £. 18,911,520, as may be found, from the detailed statement of the amount of Bank notes, and Bank Post Bills, throughout the year 1809, given in the Appx. to their Report, N° 37.

| | |
|---|---|
| The real average amount of Bank notes, exclusive of Post Bills, in 1809, was only - | £. 18,015,700 |
| The real average of the same in 1798 was - - - - - - | 12,695,970 |
| | £. 5,319,730 |

So that, the real increase of Bank notes, in 12 years, from 1798, to 1809, inclusive, was only £. 5,319,730, while the erroneous statement, which is given, by the Committee, exhibits an increase of £. 6,657,138, being an error, in excess, of £. 1,337,408; and giving, of course, to this great amount, a false view of the increase of Bank notes, in those 12 years.

If we compare the increase of Bank notes, from 1798 to 1809, with the increase, in the commerce of the country, during the same period, we shall see, that the increase of Bank notes does not come up to the increase of commerce*. If we compare the increase of Bank notes, with the increase of the revenue, and expenditure, during the same period, the

* See the Appx. N° 2, of these Considerations.

result

result is much more striking, and shows that, the increase of Bank notes is very far short, in proportion, to the increase in the revenue and expenditure of the country.

If the increase of Bank notes had even exceeded, in proportion, the increase in the commerce, and in the revenue, and expenditure of the country, it would by no means have proved an excess in the amount of Bank notes: For, of £.5,319,730, the whole increase, in the 12 years, from 1798 to 1809, no less than £.4,841,800 are small notes of one, and two pounds, leaving only an increase of the larger notes, to the amount of £.477,930, less than half a million. The above amount of small notes was plainly issued, to supply the defect of the gold coin, which had been withdrawn, from circulation. In 1798, there was of gold coin, in circulation, upwards of £.20,000,000*, which has almost disappeared from circulation; and there has, during the 11 years from 1799 to 1809, been a deficiency, in the gold coinage, to the amount of nearly £.19,000,000†. This

* The Coin Report, in 1798, supposes, that the gold coin, then in circulation, amounted to £.30,000,000. Mr. Whitmore stated, as his opinion, that the gold coin, in circulation, during the three years, previous to 1797, was rather below than above £.20,000,000. Minutes of Evidence, p. 121.

† In the 11 years, from 1788 to 1798, inclusive, the gold coined, amounted to - - - - - £.22,716,060

In the 11 years, from 1799 to 1809, inclusive, the gold coined, amounted to - - - 3,972,312

The deficiency in the last 11 years is - £.18,743,748

to

vast vacuum, in the circulating specie, would justify a much greater amount, than £.4,841,800 of small Bank notes, as a substitute, for the gold coins. From the foregoing facts, then, and accurate estimates, I submit to the judgment of all intelligent readers, whether there be, as the Committee supposes, any real excess of Bank cash, whatever there may be of Country-bank paper.

(4.) We are now come, at length, to the ultimate point of the Committee's recommendation, namely, a repeal of those Statutes, for continuing, and enforcing the Bank restriction, which the wisdom of Parliament enacted, after a just consideration, at several periods, of our existing circumstances, commercial, political, and hostile, with such an enemy. But, such a recommendation may be opposed, by the following considerations. (1.) Whatever there may be in the Committee's theory, arising from abstract reasonings, the free, and intelligent people of this nation are not governed, by abstract reasonings or metaphysical theories; but by the most practical expedients of prudent government, from a consideration of existing circumstances. (2.) Neither does our balanced Legislature ever enact laws, for the rule of the most intelligent people on earth, from abstract reasonings, or metaphysical theories: Such is the invariable wisdom of our Parliament, that it does not enact, for such a people, the best possible laws; but, the best possible laws, all circumstances regarded

which

which the people are willing to receive: For, such is our happiness, that both the Executive Government and the Legislative Power, are ultimately guided, by the VOICE OF THE PEOPLE. (3.) Then, the enquiry must be, whether the woollen manufacturers of Yorkshire, the cotton manufacturers of Lancashire, the iron manufactures of Warwickshire, the linen manufacturers of Scotland, and of Ireland, will be willing to receive any law, which goes to impede the circulation of a manufacturing people, which is the greatest evil, that can afflict them. (4.) On this head may be submitted, to the more judicious readers, the following evidence, which has been laid, at various periods, before the successive Committees of Parliament: Mr. Whitmore the Governor, and Mr. Pearce, the Deputy Governor of the Bank, stated to the Committee, that the restriction of payments, in specie, in 1797, was a much wiser, measure, than that the Bank should have persevered, in diminishing the discounts, and issues of notes, which it must have done, from a regard to its own safety, though this would have produced great public calamity, and distress. The necessity, and great benefit, are, therefore, obvious. Even before this, for a considerable time together, the discounts, and the Bank notes, were, greatly, too much restricted, and this produced great distress among the merchants, Bankers, and manufacturers;

* See Minutes of Evid. p. 110, 111, 80, 89, 95.

and

and, also, a great depression of the Government securities *. On this head; Mr. Henry Thornton stated to the Commons Committee, in 1797, that it was the *want of Bank notes*, and *not of guineas*, that was felt. Minutes, p. 139. He also stated to the Lords Committee *the benefits* which would result, *to trade, and public credit, by augmenting the quantity of Bank notes* †.

(5.) The distress among the merchants, in 1797, for want of discounts, and Bank notes, was so great, that a numerous meeting of the most respectable merchants was held, in September 1796, for the purpose of procurin grelief, by obtaining discounts, and Bank notes, on a more enlarged scale. They appointed, for this purpose, a permanent Committee, which held frequent meetings, down to the end of March 1797: and they came to various resolutions, on the subject: Among others, they declared, that "*the capital employed, in the export, and import trade of Great Britain, exclusive of the internal consumption of the country, amounted, upon an average of the last six years, to 45 millions per annum.*" A deputation of this Committee had various conferences, at different times, both with the Minister,

* See Minutes of the Lords Committee, 1797, p. 72, 78, 113, 114; and Minutes of the Commons Committee, 1797, p. 53, 68, 93, 140.

† See Minutes, p. 72—3.

and

and the Bank Directors, for the purpose of obtaining mercantile discounts, on a more enlarged scale *.

(6.) The distress, in the metropolis, and particularly among the Bankers, and merchants, was so great, for want of the necessary quantity of Bank notes, to perform the increased payments, occasioned by the increase of commerce, and manufacturers, that the Bankers, and some leading merchants, formed a plan, for relieving it, by creating any additional circulating medium: consisting of notes, which should be guaranteed, by the whole, and pass current, in the metropolis, by general consent: The Bank Charter formed, however, an obstruction to this plan †.

(7.) It was, at this epoch, of general distress, for want of the necessary quantity of circulating medium, that the restriction on payments, in specie, at the Bank was imposed; and it produced general relief, by enabling the Bank, to enlarge its discounts, and increase the issue of Bank notes. After an experience of several years, the Governor, and Deputy Governor, of the Bank stated to the late Bullion Committee, that, under existing circumstances, the restriction was found, necessary, and *experience had*

* See the Evidence of William Lushington, Esq. the Chairman of this Committee, given before the House of Commons Committee, the 6th April 1797. Minutes, p. 144, 5.

† See the Evidence of Henry Thornton, Esq. before the Lords Committee, 30th March 1797. Minutes, p. 72; and before the House of Commons Committee, 24th March, and 1st April 1797. Minutes—p. 94, 137.

*proved*

*proved, that no injury results, or is likely to result from it**. On this head; Sir Francis Baring being asked his opinion, whether any certain, and adequate, provision can be made againt an occasional excess of paper circulation, where that paper is not convertible into specie, at the option of the holder? answered: "In this country, if I may judge from experience, I should doubt it; but *if the Bank conducts itself upon the same principles, at present, when they do not pay in specie, as they did, when they were compelled, to pay in specie, I should think that it might be safely left to the discretion of the Bank*" †.

(8.) Now; the Governor, and Deputy, stated to the Committee, that the Bank does conduct themselves, on the same principles, now, as they did, before the restriction, with this beneficial difference, that not being exposed to great, and sudden, drains of specie, they are not obliged, as formerly, to make those violent contractions of their discounts, and Bank notes, in circulation, which uniformly created public distress: See the evidence of Mr. Whitmore, and Mr. Pearce, in the Minutes. They both stated, that the restriction on the Bank was, undoubtedly, no cause of the unsteadiness in the course of exchange ‡: And that the removal of the restriction

* Minutes of Evidence, p. 112 and 120.

† Ib. p. 131. ‡ Ib. p. 112.

would

would not remedy the exchange*: They, also, stated to the Committee, that the same causes, and even much stronger ones, existed, now, for the continuance of the restriction, as when it was first imposed. And they gave the strongest, and most convincing reasons, for their judgment †.

(10.) It thus appears, then, from the foregoing facts, proofs, and circumstances, that the result of the Committee's recommendation cannot be contemplated, with much satisfaction. When the Bank restriction is removed, the gold coins will only come out into circulation, to be melted, and exported. Recoinage, after recoinage, must take place, in quick succession, at an unbearable charge to the Bank, and at an enormous expence to the public. On these two topics, may be submitted to the more judicious readers what was said, by the most able Assay-master, Harris, under the two following just considerations; First, *that coinages should, in no wise, be forced*; Secondly, *that purchasing bullion, at an advanced rate, for coining, is a very weak, and insignificant measure*: On the first head, he said, " the keeping of the Mint, perpetually, at work, " seems to be the main drift of all the common " maxims, about coins; and the feeding this office " is professedly urged, as one of the reasons, for de- " basing the standard of money: And it must be " owned,

* Minutes of Evidence, p. 127. † Ib. p. 111, 125, 6.

" owned, indeed, that nothing could be more " effectual, for the compassing of that end. But, this " is proposing one evil, as a reason, for committing " another. The evils attending a general recoin- " age, which this scheme would inevitably bring " about, are many, and great; but without entering " into a detail of those evils, at present, let it here " suffice, to examine into the merits of that notion, " which is, very generally, entertained, that coinages " are, by all means to be encouraged.

" In one sense, coinage is a neutral, harmless, " and indifferent act; for if it be left free, it nei- " ther enriches, nor impoverishes, the nation, one " single penny; the coins just pay, for the bullion " whereof they were made, and the profits to the " Mint are spent amongst themselves. But, it " deserves well to be considered, that coining is, " nevertheless, an act of very great importance: " That a very great trust is thereby lodged in the " Mint; that it requires very great care, and great " skill too, in those intrusted, to keep exactly to " the standard; that a small deviation from it upon " each piece, would soon amount to a large sum; " that coins are universal pledges; and that the " credit of nations is greatly concerned, in the ex- " actness, and faithfulness of their Mints. When " these things are considered, will it follow, that " coinages are to be promoted unnecessarily? " That coins once faithfully made of their due

" fineness

"fineness are to be melted into the unattested "state of bullion, for no other purpose, than to be "recoined again?"

And, on the *second* head, he said, "besides "debasing the standard, another expedient hath "been hit upon, for feeding the Mint; and that is, "the purchasing of bullion, at an advanced price, "for coining, or the giving more per ounce, for the "bullion, than it would be afterwards worth, in "coin. But, although this measure is very harm-"less, as to any consequences attending it, except-"ing to those immediately concerned; yet it cannot "be reckoned a very wise one: For, whatever be "the cause, that prevents bullion, from coming into "the Mint; whilst that cause subsists, and coining "will not remove it, the new coins will be melted "into bullion again, and again coined; and so round "in a circle, as long as a *premium* to the importer of "bullion into the Mint, is continued. And, after "all this expence, and all the expectation raised "from it, no new coins will be to be seen; the "same cause, that created a scarcity before, will "carry all these away; and nothing will be left, "but the gains, that had been made at the Mint. "After what hath been said here, and in the pre-"ceding, it might be asked, of what use, then, is "the Mint? To which, I answer, that a Mint, "rightly established, is a very useful, necessary, "and important office; an office, that those at the "head

"head of our finances should have due cognizance "of, as being answerable to the public, that its "operations are faithfully performed. The natural "waste, and dissipation of coins, require frequent "supplies. This, trade, naturally, and abundantly, "furnishes; and this vent for its bullion, when "other markets do not invite, is also of very great "advantage to trade; it prevents a stagnation, and "uncertainty, in a very considerable branch of "commerce. No Mint can be kept constantly at "work, unless coining becomes a kind of manu- "factory, for foreign commerce; which is not the "case here, nor could it be, without very great loss "to us, upon our present Mint establishment. But, "the Mint, if left free to its own natural course, "cannot fail of keeping up the national coins to "their due quantity; what it does more, may be "truly said to be labour lost; and would prove "mischievous, if trade did not step in, and sweep "away the superfluous coin. What hath been "here said, regards coining in general; without re- "specting the disparagements, which either silver, "or gold coins may lie under, in particular, at the "Mint; and it may serve, as a full answer, to those, "who are for promoting coinages, by forced, and un- "natural methods*." Thus far, the greatest Assay-master, and one of the ablest writers of his enlightened age! The Committee has, indeed, referred to the great recoinage of silver, in King William's reign, as a proper precedent,

* Essay on Money, 66—9.

cedent, for the coming recoinage, after recoinage of the gold. Of Mr. Montague, the Chancellor of the Exchequer, who carried through King William's recoinage of silver, it is recorded, that he *avowed* on that pressing occasion, "that he would *rather* "do *mischief* than *nothing*." Let us hope, however, that the political wisdom of the present times will say to all theoretical projectors, that it is *much better, to do nothing*, than *michief*. Of the vast charge to the public, for King William's coinage, and what disappointment was, in the result, need not be again told; of what a sacrifice of justice to theory, of the poor to the rich, was made, when Mr. Montague did mischief, rather than nothing, Sir James Stuart has clearly shown *.—All will be safe, and sure, when the well-informed voice of the people cries out, in the sentiment, and language, of ADDISON,

"True fortitude is seen, in great exploits,
"That justice warrants, and that wisdom guides;
"All else is towering frenzy, and distraction."

---

* Political Economy.

Appendix,

# APPENDIX:

*VIZ.*

N°

I.—A Chronological Account of COMMERCE, in this Island, from the Restoration, to the year 1809, inclusive.

II.—A *Comparative* State, in *ten* columns; showing, *when*, and on what *Motives*, were issued The BANK NOTES; &c. &c.

III.—On COUNTRY BANKS; in three sections.

# APPENDIX.

## Appendix, N III.

FAR, from me, be the wish, of interrupting any one's business, of hurting any one's feelings, or of disparaging establishments, which may have done good, and may be made salutary. But, the best things; the most sanctified, and most valuable of all things, such as *religion* and *liberty*, are liable to the worst abuses of superstition, and licentiousness: Thus, are more than *seven hundred* Country Banks a *prodigious abuse*. I am aware, however, that among so great a number, there are many of solid capitals, and great respectability: We might infer as much, from the Evidence of Mr. *Richardson*, who speaks of a system of *discounts*, by the *Eastern* Country Banks, for the Western traders, which are of great amount, and real usefulness, to the commercial world; and from Mr. T. Thomson's Evidence, which shows, that there are Northern Country Banks, whose notes are taken, by the people, in preference to *Bank notes*, themselves. Yet, after fully investigating the whole subject, of the Bullion Committee's Enquiries, and Report, I am fully satisfied, that there is no real abuse, in the whole Banking system, and accustomed practice of Great Britain, (with those of Ireland I meddle *not)* but, in the Country Banks, of England, which

which appear to me, to be too many, too obscure, and too unsafe, for such a nation. Some years ago, when I had this weighty subject before me, the two following papers were communicated to me, from a respectable quarter, which lay open some of the *management*, and artifices, in so striking a view, that I thought it, for the public benefit, to publish them, in this supplementary Appendix.

—— i. ——

INSTRUCTIONS from a Banking House, in London, to their Clerks, on their departure, from Town, to open certain BANKS, in the Country.

YOU are authorized by us to manage a Bank at ——— under the firm of ———.

The business to be, an exchange of paper, for which you are to charge ¼ per cent. stamp and postage, and draw on the house of ——— Bankers, London; and all bills so drawn, are to be signed in the name of ——— only for the above firm.

One guinea notes to be issued, and ¼ per cent. allowed to all those, who undertake to keep them out a month.

Good bills may be discounted, and cash notes given for them, only at such times as you have a surplus of cash in the Bank.

Also at all times you may discount London bills, giving in exchange for them, drafts on our house at 21 *D. D.* * sending such bills up to us per first post.

You may also discount bills payable at ——— giving your shop notes for the same, but this must be done with caution; and if you are not sufficiently acquainted with the responsibility of the persons bringing such bill, they must bring a person who will be accountable, or get the same indorsed by a respectable person residing on the spot.

You must at all times *keep the house in London in cash*, avoiding as much as possible, throwing them into any advances.

No person to have shop notes to issue, unless leaving cash or Bank notes for the same.

You are not to advance any money on account, unless authorized by the house in London to do it.

You are to get as many accounts opened as possibly you can from the Riders, giving them drafts on us for the same, and if any expences attend the same, you must charge it to the account of disbursements; also whatever expences attend going from ——— to any place, on account of the house, to be charged.

If, at any period, any merchant or tradesman wishes to alter this mode of doing business from the above plan laid down by us, you must acquaint the house in London, and have their approbation for the same.

* Is not this usury?

We

We expect that you strictly follow the above rules, keeping the Bank open for doing business the same hours as other Banks.

All notes and drafts to be drawn dated ——— payable in London only.

Provided merchants or tradesmen open accounts with cash, Bank notes, or other cash notes, such person to have shop notes, or cash, allowed them at such times as they require it.

[Signed by the first Partner for the Firm.]

---

Extract of a Letter from the Managing Clerk, to *M. A.*

" On the 6th of July, I opened a Bank at ———
" and continued there fourteen days without one
" guinea to commence with, since which I have
" opened the Bank at ——— without a single
" farthing. There is nothing doing at either house;
" and we are d——d by the people here :—I am
" at present behind the counter, not capable of
" giving cash for a single Bank note."

—— ii. ——

Copy of a LETTER, dated, at Bristol, on the 25th of January, 1802, from T. K. to S. T. in London.

SIR,

I consider myself highly honoured by your Secretary's reply to my letter, under date 23d May; and as I have been informed that there is a Bill preparing,

paring, for the regulation of Country Banks, I take the liberty of troubling you with the following information: should it prove in the slightest degree serviceable, it will give me much pleasure. I have kept back the firm of the house, but, under the seal of honour, if thought necessary, it shall be disclosed.

I was some time since applied to by a house in London, to superintend, once a week, a Banking concern, which was about to be established, in Bath; concluding every thing fair, I agreed with the party, but, to my astonishment, when I went over and asked the managing Clerk what was the amount, in *cash* or *Bank* of *England* notes, with which he intended to open, his answer was, that he had not a single guinea; but had brought a bundle of blanks, which he was to sign for the firm, and with those alone, he was to raise a capital, as engagements had been made with people in the town, to circulate them, and return, in lieu thereof *cash* or *Bank* notes, for which they were to receive ¼ per cent. I beg'd leave to withdraw from so *honourable* an employment, and the plan was abandoned: Since which, I received a letter, from the managing Clerk, with copy of orders, for opening sundry Banks, in the North, requesting my opinion of the same; and as I conceive the whole to be a grand scheme of swindling, I do not consider it any breach of honour to inclose you copy thereof. I have also been offered ¼ per cent.

if

if I would undertake to circulate their notes, but of course declined it.

Some time since a parner, in one of the first houses, in this city, told me he had made application to a country grocer, for a debt of a few hundred pounds, whose answer was, that he could not then pay, but that as he was going to open a Bank very shortly, he would make an early remittance. The bank was opened—The remittance was made. The increasing evil of Bankers of this description calls aloud upon the Bank of England, to interfere, and provide, a remedy, and it merits their most serious consideration.

If £. 10,000, or £. 20,000, were to be deposited, by every country, and town Bank, also in the Bank of England, would it not effectually prevent men of straw, and swindlers, from thus imposing on the public?

A circumstance happened at Wells, just before the failure of the Banking concern there, which will shew how much confidence was placed by the country in them. A farmer received a Bank note drawn in favour of Mr. Newland, and brought it to the Wells Bank, to get one of their notes for it, observing, he knew nothing of Abraham Newland, but he knew Master Bobby, there, pointing to Mr. Robt. ———, one of the partners: every endeavour was made to persuade him to hold it, to no purpose. Their failure a few days after afforded him an oppor-

tunity

tunity of judging more correctly which was best.—In America, I have seen the best consequences flow, from the establishment of what are there term'd *Branch* Banks, or Banks branched off from the great National Bank, at Philadelphia, who have their Governors and Committees, of course, subservient to the principal; how far the adoption of such a plan, in England, would answer, you are best judge; but, something ought to be done, to put a stop to practices, big with the fate of the trading part of society.

I hope you will have the goodness to pardon this intrusion; my intentions are pure, and if my communications have little worth, they have at least truth for their basis.—But should you consider any part of them worth the attention of your highly respectable Committee, I must beg the favour, that my name may not be mentioned.—I am in a public line, here, as Accountant and Broker, and if it were known, that I was the author of this address, it might be a very serious injury to me; although it ought not, for there is not a Bank in this city, but what is of the first respectability.

I am, &c.

T. K.

P. S. I am happy to say, Sir, your stamping the forged Notes has given universal satisfaction; as well as the publication of the Clerks' names.

— iii. —

With regard to the COUNTRY BANKS, the following *points* seem to have been laid before the BULLION COMMITTEE, in Evidence: (1.) As to the *principle* of their *issues*; (2.) The *amount* of their *Notes*; (3.) Their OPTIONAL CLAUSES; (4.) Their *modes* of *lending Money*; (5.) Their *Discounts*; (6.) Their *Comparative Stability*; and (7.) The *numbers*, at *succesive periods*.

1. As to *the* PRINCIPLE of *their issues*; Mr. Stuckey a partner, in three Banks, at Bristol, Bridgewater, and Langport, in Somersetshire, stated, that *they regulate their issues of notes, by the assets they have, in London, to pay them, without much reference to the quantity of Bank of England notes*, or *specie, which we have*, although we always keep a quantity of both the latter, in our coffers, to pay occasional demands, made in the Country *. He said, they keep only a small quantity of Bank of England notes; but a large proportion of guineas: They pay their notes partly in guineas †.

2. With regard to the *amount* of *their notes*; the *Country Bank* notes, in circulation, decreased considerably, between 1793 and 1797 ‡. In 1810, their

* Minutes of Evidence, p. 140. † Ib. p. 139.

‡ See the Evidence of Henry Thornton, Esq. before the Lords Committee, 1797. Minutes 74—5.

notes,

notes, in circulation, were supposed, to amount to 20 *millions, including Scotland**. John Henry Tritton, Banker, London, concurred †. Mr. Richardson, the Bill-broker, said, "I have heard it calculated at 30 millions, (including Scotland) ‡. Mr. Gilchrist supposes the notes, in Scotland, amount to, from 2 to 2½ millions §.

3. With regard to the *optional Clauses*; Mr. Richardson said, that the Country *Bank notes, with optional Clauses*, to be paid, at the Bank, or in London, *have greatly increased, during several years past* ||.

4. With regard to the *mode of lending Money*; Mr. Stuckey, before mentioned, said, "We are not "fond of lending upon mortgage, and seldom do "it; we generally issue our notes, by discounting "good bills, or by lending cash, for a short period, "to agriculturists, upon their own security, or the "best, that we may think proper ¶.

With regard to their *Discounts*; Mr. Thomas Richardson, the Bill-broker, and *Agent*, for *Country Banks*, said, that he negociates *the discount of bills, with the Country Banks*, to the amount of

* Before the Commons Committee, 1797.—Minutes, p. 133—4; of Thomas Thompson, Esq. before the Bullion Committee, Minutes p. 95—6—7. And the Evidence of Mr. Ellison before the Lords Committee, 1797, Minutes, p. 88.

† Minutes of Bullion Committee, p. 140.

‡ Minutes of Bullion Committee, p. 149. § Ib. p. 113.

|| Ib. 122: Mr. Tritton concurred, Ib. 141. ¶ Ib. p. 139.

*seven,*

*seven, or eight millions, in the course of a year.* Several other persons do *about a third as much more,* [making in all about *ten millions*]*. Most of these bills are sent, from various parts of the Country, up to London; and transmitted by him to various Country Banks, in different parts, for discount†; he also said he sent *London bills, to the Country Banks for discount.* Of the whole bills, thus discounted, by the Country Banks, at least *two thirds of them are such as the Bank of England would refuse to discount, on account of their having more than 65 days to run*‡: This practice of discounting, with the Country Banks, prevailed previous to the restriction§. The sums of money, which *he lends for Country Bankers, on discount, are 50 times more, than the sums borrowed for Country Bankers*‖. On this great discount of bills, by the Country Banks, there have been but very small losses of late. There were *many more losses, in proportion, before the Bank restriction*¶.

6. With regard to their stability; Thomas Thompson, Esq. stated, that *there have been fewer interruptions to the credit of Country-bank paper, since the suspension of payments, at the Bank, than there were before***. Mr. Tritton said, that, by the removal of the restriction, the Country Banks would be more liable to a run on them ††.

* Minutes, p. 123, 125. † Ib. p. 122. ‡ Ib. p. 123.
§ Ib. p. 123. ‖ Ib. p. 122. ¶ Ib. p, 124.
** Minutes p. 115. †† Ib. p. 141.

With

7. With regard to *their Number*; it was said that, their number decreased, from about 280, in the beginning of 1793, to about 230, in the beginning of 1797*. In 1808, there were some more than 600: By the list lately published (1810) there appears to be 721†. But, both these numbers in 1808, & 1810, are incorrect; as they include all the Banks, and branches of Banks, in Scotland; and count some twice over. The Country Banks have increased 100, within the last *two* years: In 1810, the number of Country Banks, in England, and Wales, were 646, including, 2 in Berwick, 3 *in Guernsey*, 2 in Jersey, and, 1 *in the Isle of Man*. In 1810, the number of *Banks*, in Scotland, were 36; of this 36, there are 13 in Edinburgh; viz. 3 chartered Banks, and 10 others; and the number of *branches is somewhat more*; *in all about* 83. In 1810, the total number in Britain, exclusive of London, was 729; there were then in London 66‡. But, the *subjoined Document* will be found more specific, and satisfactory.

* Evidence of Mr. Ellison, Agent for the Country Banks, Minutes of Lords Committee, 1797, p. 87.

† Evidence of Mr. Tritton, Minutes Bullion Committee, 140.

‡ See the Evidence throughout.

A STATEMENT of the Numbers, and Places, of the Banks of England, Wales, and Scotland; distinguishing the *Numbers*, with the *Population*, in each District. [From the *printed List*, 1810, and other Authorities.]

| | Banks in 1810. | Population in 1801. | | Banks in 1810. | Population in 1801. |
|---|---|---|---|---|---|
| Bedfordshire - - | 4 | 63,393 | Middlesex, exclusive of London and Westminster | 2 | 89,567 |
| Berkshire - - | 15 | 109,215 | | | |
| Buckinghamshire - | 6 | 107,444 | Monmouthshire - | 4 | 45,582 |
| Cambridgeshire - | 10 | 89,346 | Norfolk - - - | 17 | 273,371 |
| Cheshire - - - | 10 | 191,751 | Northamptonshire - | 8 | 131,757 |
| Cornwall - - - | 20 | 188,269 | Northumberland - | 5 | 149,914 |
| Cumberland - - | 12 | 117,230 | Nottinghamshire - | 12 | 140,350 |
| Derbyshire - - | 11 | 161,142 | Oxfordshire - - | 14 | 109,620 |
| Devonshire - - | 35 | 343,001 | Rutland - - - | 2 | 16,356 |
| Dorsetshire - - | 15 | 115,319 | Shropshire - - | 21 | 167,639 |
| Durham - - - | 8 | 160,361 | Somerset - - - | 34 | 273,750 |
| Essex - - - | 13 | 226,437 | Staffordshire - - | 21 | 259,153 |
| Gloucestershire - | 34 | 250,809 | Suffolk - - - | 13 | 210,431 |
| Hampshire - - | 30 | 219,656 | Surrey, exclusive of Southwark - - | 14 | 201,595 |
| Herefordshire - - | 6 | 89,191 | | | |
| Hertfordshire - - | 10 | 97,577 | Sussex - - - | 20 | 159,311 |
| Huntingdonshire - | 3 | 37,568 | Warwickshire - - | 20 | 208,190 |
| Kent - - - | 31 | 307,624 | Westmorland - - | 2 | 41,617 |
| Lancashire - - | 15 | 672,731 | Wiltshire - - - | 17 | 185,107 |
| Leicestershire - - | 11 | 130,081 | Worcestershire - | 13 | 139,333 |
| Lincolnshire - - | 21 | 208,557 | Yorkshire - - | 54 | 858,892 |

| | Banks | Population |
|---|---|---|
| The Total, in England - - - | 613 | 7,548,237 |
| The Total, in Wales - - - | 25 | 541,546 |
| The Total, in England, and Wales - | 638 | 8,089,783 |
| In Berwick on Tweed - - - - - - - | 2 | 7,187 |
| | 640 | 8,096,970 |
| In London, Westminster, and Southwark; being 66 Bankers; and The BANK of ENGLAND - - - | 67 | 877,876 |
| The Total - - | 707 | 8,974,846 |
| In the Isle of Man - - - - - - - - | 1 | — |
| In Guernsey - - - - - - - - - | 3 | — |
| In Jersey - - - - - - - - - | 2 | — |
| The general Total of all those Districts - | 713 | 8,974,846 |
| - - D° - - of Scotland - - - | 83 | 1,618,303 |
| The Grand Total - - | 796 | 10,593,149 |

THE

## The RECAPITULATION of ENGLAND.

| | | Banks in 1810. | Population in 1801. |
|---|---|---|---|
| Bedfordshire - - | Bedford Town - - - | 1 | 3,948 |
| | Biggleswade - - - - | 2 | 1,650 |
| | Luton - - - - - | 1 | 3,095 |
| | Total in Bedfordshire - | 4 | 63,393 |
| Berkshire - - - | Reading Town - - - | 2 | 9,742 |
| | Abingdon - - - - | 4 | 4,356 |
| | Windsor - - - - | 2 | 4,793 |
| | Newbury - - - - | 2 | 4,275 |
| | Wallingford - - - - | 2 | 1,744 |
| | Other Banks in Berkshire - | 3 | — |
| | Total in Berkshire - - | 15 | 109,215 |
| Buckinghamshire - | Buckingham Town - - | 1 | 2,605 |
| | Aylesbury - - - - | 2 | 3,186 |
| | Other Banks in Buckinghamshire - - - - | 3 | — |
| | Total in Buckinghamshire | 6 | 107,444 |
| Cambridgeshire - | Cambridge Town - - - | 3 | 10,087 |
| | Other Banks in Cambridgeshire | 7 | — |
| | Total in Cambridgeshire - | 10 | 89,346 |
| Cheshire - - - | Chester City - - - | 2 | 15,052 |
| | Macclesfield Town - - | 2 | 8,743 |
| | Other Banks in Cheshire - | 6 | — |
| | Total in Cheshire - - | 10 | 191,751 |

Cornwall

| | | Banks in 1810. | Population in 1801. |
|---|---|---|---|
| Cornwall - - - | Launceston the County Town - | 2 | 1,483 |
| | Falmouth - - - - - | 3 | 3,684 |
| | Other Banks in Cornwall - | 15 | — |
| | Total in Cornwall - - | 20 | 188,269 |
| Cumberland - - | Carlisle Town - - - - | 4 | 10,255 |
| | Whitehaven - - - - - | 3 | 8,742 |
| | Workington - - - - - | 2 | 5,716 |
| | Other Banks in Cumberland - | 3 | — |
| | Total in Cumberland - | 12 | 117,230 |
| Derbyshire - - | Derby Town - - - - | 4 | 10,832 |
| | Other Banks in Derbyshire - | 7 | — |
| | Total in Derbyshire - | 11 | 161,142 |
| Devonshire - - | Exeter City - - - - | 6 | 17,412 |
| | Plymouth Town - - - | 7 | 43,194 |
| | Other Banks in Devonshire - | 22 | — |
| | Total in Devonshire - | 35 | 343,001 |
| Dorsetshire - - | Dorchester, the County Town | 1 | 2,402 |
| | Poole - - - - - - | 2 | 4,761 |
| | Weymouth - - - - - | 2 | 3,617 |
| | Bridport - - - - - | 2 | 3,117 |
| | Blandford - - - - - | 2 | 2,326 |
| | Other Banks in Dorsetshire - | 6 | — |
| | Total in Dorsetshire - | 15 | 115,319 |
| Durham - - - | Durham City - - - - | 1 | 7,530 |
| | Sunderland Town - - - - | 2 | 12,412 |
| | Stockton - - - - - | 3 | 4,009 |
| | Darlington - - - - - | 2 | 4,670 |
| | Total in Durham County | 8 | 160,361 |

Essex

| | | Banks in 1810. | Population in 1801. |
|---|---|---|---|
| Essex - - - | Colchester - - - - | 2 | 11,520 |
| | Chelmsford - - - - | 2 | 3,755 |
| | Other Banks in Essex - - | 9 | — |
| | Total in Essex - - | 13 | 226,437 |
| Glocestershire - | Glocester City - - - | 4 | 7,579 |
| | Bristol City - - - | 11 | 63,645 |
| | Tewkesbury Town - - | 2 | 4,199 |
| | Cirencester - - - - | 2 | 4,130 |
| | Other Banks in Glocestershire | 15 | — |
| | Total in Glocestershire - | 34 | 250,809 |
| Herefordshire - | Hereford City - - - | 2 | 6,828 |
| | Other Banks in Herefordshire | 4 | — |
| | Total in Herefordshire - | 6 | 89,191 |
| Hertfordshire - | Hertford Town - - - | 1 | 3,360 |
| | St. Albans - - - - | 1 | 3,038 |
| | Other Banks in Hertfordshire | 8 | — |
| | Total in Hertfordshire - | 10 | 97,577 |
| Huntingdonshire - | Huntingdon Town - - | 2 | 2,035 |
| | St. Neots - - - - | 1 | 1,752 |
| | Total in Huntingdonshire - | 3 | 37,568 |
| Kent - - - - | Canterbury City - - - | 2 | 9,000 |
| | Rochester City - - - | 1 | 6,817 |
| | Dover Town - - - | 2 | 14,845 |
| | Maidstone - - - - | 3 | 8,027 |
| | Deal - - - - - | 2 | 5,420 |
| | Faversham - - - - | 2 | 3,364 |
| | Ramsgate - - - - | 2 | 3,110 |
| | Gravesend - - - - | 2 | 2,483 |
| | Other Banks in Kent - - | 15 | — |
| | Total in Kent - - - | 31 | 307,024 |

| County | Place | Banks in 1810. | Population in 1801. |
|---|---|---|---|
| Lancashire - - | Lancaster the County Town - | 2 | 9,030 |
| | Manchester - - - - | 2 | 84,020 |
| | Liverpool - - - - | 5 | 77,653 |
| | Wigan - - - - - | 2 | 10,989 |
| | Other Banks in Lancashire - | 4 | — |
| | Total in Lancashire - - | 15 | 672,731 |
| Leicestershire - | - Leicester Town - - - | 3 | 16,953 |
| | Other Banks in Leicestershire - | 8 | |
| | Total in Lecestershire - - | 11 | 130,081 |
| Lincolnshire - | - Lincoln City - - - | 2 | 7,398 |
| | Grantham Town - - - | 2 | 7,014 |
| | Boston - - - - | 6 | 5,926 |
| | Stamford - - - - | 3 | 4,022 |
| | Other Banks in Lincolnshire - | 8 | — |
| | Total in Lincolnshire - - | 21 | 208,557 |
| Middlesex - - | - Uxbridge - - - - | 1 | 2,111 |
| | Staines - - - - | 1 | 1,750 |
| | Total, exclusive of London and Westminster - - | 2 | 89,567 |
| | Monmouthshire Total - | 4 | 45,582 |
| Norfolk - - - | - Norwich City - - - | 5 | 36,854 |
| | Yarmouth Town - - - | 2 | 14,845 |
| | Lynn Regis - - - - | 2 | 10,096 |
| | Other Banks in Norfolk - - | 8 | — |
| | Total in Norfolk - - | 17 | 273,371 |

Northamptonshire

| | | Banks in 1810. | Population in 1801. |
|---|---|---|---|
| Northamptonshire | Northampton Town - - | 1 | 7,020 |
| | Peterborough City - - | 2 | 3,449 |
| | Other Banks in Northamptonshire - - - - - | 5 | — |
| | Total in Northamptonshire | 8 | 131,757 |
| Northumberland - | Newcastle-on-Tyne - - | 4 | 28,366 |
| | Morpeth - - - - - | 1 | 2,951 |
| | Total in Northumberland | 5 | 149,914 |
| Nottinghamshire - | Nottingham Town - - | 6 | 28,861 |
| | Newark - - - - - | 2 | 6,730 |
| | Other Banks in this Shire - | 4 | — |
| | Total in Nottinghamshire | 12 | 140,350 |
| Oxfordshire - - | Oxford City - - - | 4 | 11,694 |
| | Henley Town - - - | 2 | 2,948 |
| | Chipping Norton - - - | 2 | 1,812 |
| | Other Banks in this Shire - | 6 | — |
| | Total in Oxfordshire - | 14 | 109,620 |
| Rutland - - - - - | - Total - - | 2 | 16,356 |
| Shropshire - - | Shrewsbury County Town - | 3 | 14,739 |
| | Wellington - - - - - | 3 | 7,531 |
| | Bridgenorth - - - - - | 2 | 4,408 |
| | Ludlow - - - - - | 2 | 3,897 |
| | Other Banks in Shropshire - | 11 | — |
| | Total in Shropshire - | 21 | 167,639 |

Somerset

| County | Town | Banks in 1810. | Population in 1801. |
|---|---|---|---|
| Somerset - - - | Bath City - - - - - | 6 | 27,700 |
| | Taunton Town - - - | 3 | 5,794 |
| | Bridgewater - - - | 3 | 3,634 |
| | Wincanton - - - - - | 3 | 1,772 |
| | Wellington - - - - | 3 | 4,033 |
| | Yeovil - - - - - | 3 | 2,774 |
| | Frome - - - - - | 2 | 8,748 |
| | Other Banks in this Shire - | 11 | — |
| | Total in Somersetshire - | 34 | 273,750 |
| Hampshire - - | Winchester City - - - | 3 | 6,069 |
| | Southampton Town - - | 3 | 7,913 |
| | Portsmouth and Portsea - - | 3 | 32,166 |
| | Ringwood - - - - - | 2 | 3,222 |
| | Andover - - - - - | 2 | 3,304 |
| | Basingstoke - - - - | 2 | 2,589 |
| | Lymington - - - - | 2 | 2,378 |
| | Isle of Wight - - - | 4 | 22,097 |
| | Other Banks in this Shire - | 9 | — |
| | Total in Hampshire - | 30 | 219,656 |
| Staffordshire - - | Litchfield City - - - | 2 | 4,512 |
| | Stafford Town - - - | 3 | 3,898 |
| | Wolverhampton - - - | 3 | 12,565 |
| | Walsall - - - - - | 2 | 5,177 |
| | Uttoxeter - - - - - | 3 | 2,779 |
| | Other Banks in this Shire - | 8 | — |
| | Total in Staffordshire - | 21 | 239,153 |
| Suffolk - - - | Ipswich, the County Town - | 2 | 11,277 |
| | Bury St. Edmund's - - | 3 | 7,655 |
| | Stowmarket - - - | 2 | 1,761 |
| | Other Banks in Suffolk - - | 6 | — |
| | Total in Suffolk - - | 13 | 210,431 |

| | | Banks in 1801. | Population in 1801. |
|---|---|---|---|
| Surrey - - - | Guildford, the County Town - | 2 | 2,634 |
| | Croydon - - - - - | 4 | 5,743 |
| | Farnham - - - - | 2 | 2,508 |
| | Other Banks in Surrey - - | 6 | — |
| | Total in Surrey, exclusive of Southwark - - | 14 | 201,595 |
| Suffex - - - - | Chichester City - - - | 3 | 4,744 |
| | Brighthelmston - - - | 3 | 7,339 |
| | Lewes - - - - - | 2 | 3,309 |
| | Arundel - - - - | 2 | 1,855 |
| | Worthing - - - - | 2 | — |
| | Other Banks in this Shire - | 8 | — |
| | Total in Sussex - - | 20 | 159,311 |
| Warwickshire - | Coventry City - - - | 5 | 16,049 |
| | Warwick Town - - - | 3 | 5,775 |
| | Birmingham - - - | 7 | 73,670 |
| | Other Banks in this Shire - | 5 | — |
| | Total in Warwickshire - | 20 | 208,190 |
| Westmoreland - | Kendal - - - - - | 2 | 6,892 |
| | Total in Westmoreland - | 2 | 41,617 |
| Wiltshire - - | Salisbury City - - - | 2 | 7,668 |
| | Devizes Town - - - | 2 | 7,909 |
| | Warminster - - - | 2 | 4,932 |
| | Chippenham - - - | 2 | 3,366 |
| | Marlborough - - - | 2 | 2,367 |
| | Other Banks in this Shire - | 7 | — |
| | Total in Wiltshire - - | 17 | 185,107 |

Worcestershire

| | | Banks in 1810. | Population in 1801. |
|---|---|---|---|
| Worcestershire - | Worcester City - - - | 2 | 11,470 |
| | Dudley Town - - - | 2 | 10,107 |
| | Kidderminster - - - | 2 | 6,110 |
| | Bewdley - - - - | 2 | 3,671 |
| | Stourbridge - - - | 2 | 3,431 |
| | Other Banks in this Shire - | 3 | — |
| | Total in Worcestershire - | 13 | 139,333 |
| Yorkshire - - | York City - - - - - | 2 | 16,145 |
| | Leeds - - - - - - | 5 | 30,669 |
| | Hull - - - - - - | 5 | 29,156 |
| | Sheffield - - - - | 2 | 31,314 |
| | Huddersfield - - - | 4 | 7,268 |
| | Whitby - - - - - | 3 | 7,483 |
| | Halifax - - - - - | 2 | 8,886 |
| | Wakefield - - - - | 2 | 8,131 |
| | Malton - - - - - | 3 | 3,788 |
| | Rippon - - - - - | 3 | 3,211 |
| | Pontefract - - - - | 3 | 3,144 |
| | Doncaster - - - - | 2 | 5,697 |
| | Scarborough - - - | 2 | 6,688 |
| | Beverley - - - - | 2 | 5,401 |
| | Knaresborough - - - | 2 | 3,388 |
| | Richmond - - - - | 2 | 2,861 |
| | Other Banks in this Shire - | 10 | — |
| | Total in Yorkshire - - | 54 | 858,892 |

THE RECAPITULATION OF WALES.

| | | |
|---|---|---|
| Swansea - - - - - - - - | 3 | 6,099 |
| Carmarthen - - - - - - - - | 2 | 5,548 |
| Haverfordwest - - - - - - - | 2 | 2,880 |
| Wrexham - - - - - - - - | 2 | 2,575 |
| Other Banks, in Wales - - - - - - | 16 | — |
| | 25 | 541,546 |

## THE RECAPITULATION OF SCOTLAND.

| | Banks in 1810. | Population in 1801. |
|---|---|---|
| The *chartered* Banks in Edinburgh, - - 3<br>Other Banks, in Edinburgh, that issue notes 2<br>Bankers, in Edinburgh, that do *not* issue notes 8<br>The Leith Bank; all in Edinburghshire - 1 | 14 | 124,124 |
| Banks, in Glasgow—in Lanerkshire - - | 4 | 150,690 |
| Banks, in Dundee—in Forfarshire - - - | 3 | 99,127 |
| Banks, in Aberdeen—in Aberdeenshire - - | 2 | 122,279 |
| Banks, in Paisley - 2<br>Banks, in Greenock 2 } in Renfrewshire - | 4 | 79,891 |
| Banks, in Falkirk - 2<br>D° - - in Stirling - 1 } in Stirling-shire - | 3 | 50,825 |
| Bank, in Cupar - - 1<br>Fifeshire-Bank - - 1 } in Fife-shire - - | 2 | 93,743 |
| Bank, in Ayr - - 1<br>Bank, in Kilmarnock 1 } in Ayr-shire - - | 2 | 84,206 |
| Bank, in Perth - - in Perth-shire - - | 1 | 126,466 |
| Galloway-Bank - - in Kircudbright Stewartry - | 1 | 29,211 |
| The Total of the Banks, in SCOTLAND - | 36 | |
| Of those 36, about 22 issue notes: There are<br>Branches of the Bank of Scotland - - 20<br>At Glasgow, a Branch of the Royal Bank - 1<br>Branches of the British Linen Company - 15 | | |
| Total Branches of the Chartered Banks - 36<br>Branches of the Dundee, Aberdeen, and Glasgow Banks - - - - 11 | 47 | |
| The whole Banks, and Branches, in Scotland | 83 | 1,618,303 |

FINIS.